Clinical Depression and the Stalker Within

I0104031

Dr. Francisco Talavera

Chipmunkapublishing
the mental health publisher

Published by

Chipmunkapublishing

http://www.chipmunkapublishing.com

Copyright © Francisco Talavera 2013

ISBN   978-1-84991-962-3

Chipmunkapublishing gratefully acknowledge the support of Arts Council England.

Biography of Francisco Talavera:

Born in 1957 Dr. Talavera struggled with clinical depression at an early age. Just when he thought he had reached the end of the road and survived a suicide attempt, he was able to put his life back together. Although he continued to struggle with depression he managed to finish a master's degree in science at North Dakota State University and a doctoral degree in science at Washington State University. He then went on to pursue a postdoctoral in reproductive endocrinology and oncology at the University of Michigan. Throughout his graduate work he also published several scientific articles in well respected peer reviewed journals. Following his postdoctoral training he pursued a doctorate degree in pharmacy at Creighton University.

He is currently Editor-in-Chief for one of the leading drug reference websites in the United States and an adjunct assistant professor at the University Of Nebraska Medical Center College Of Pharmacy. He is also the Author of Pharmacy Review, Pearls of Wisdom (Boston Medical Publishing Corporation 2001) and Rapid Fire Pharmacy Review (Jones and Bartlett Publishers 2006).

While in pursuit of his graduate work Dr. Talavera found a sense of purpose in volunteer work. He volunteered as a crisis line counselor for suicide prevention in Pullman, Washington. He then moved to Ann Arbor, Michigan, to pursue his postdoctoral work and volunteered as a counselor at Ozone House, a program that helps runaway homeless kids and taught life skills to kids living at Miller House, a group home. He also volunteered as a mentor at Project Transition, a center for the mentally challenged and worked part-time as a counselor at Dawn Farm, a detox and drug rehab program in Ypsilanti, Michigan.

The skills that he developed while doing volunteer work gave him the foundation to use techniques aimed at tackling his clinical depression and achieve a sense of peace. For the past fifteen years that sense of peace has strengthened. Today he is happily married with two beautiful kids looking forward to help others achieve the sense of peace that eludes those who feel desponded and hopelessly depressed.

Dedication

To my son Iesele and daughter Kyla, for making my world a better place

Contents

Introduction

Chapter 1.

Keeping Your Mind Simple When Facing Clinical Depression

How I Developed a Simple Mind through Awareness

A Life Gone Out of Order

Keeping your Life in Order

Letting Go

Chapter 2.

Modifying Your Beliefs and Thoughts

Productive Self-talk and Our Quality of Life

Our Culture and Our Quality of Life

Restructuring Your Self-Talk

Restructuring Feelings of Guilt

Restructuring Feelings of Failure

Understanding Success

Learning to Set Goals

Chapter 3.

Coping With Depression and Feelings of Suicide

Learning to Work with Emotions When Facing Clinical Depression

Dealing with the Anger Within

Let's Talk Suicide

Learning to Remain Productive When Experiencing Feelings of Suicide

Helping Someone who's Suicidal

Chapter 4.

A Word About Families, Their Influence on Our Emotional Strength, and Our Ability to Change

Who's Responsible for Our Ability to Change?

Chapter 5.

Medications, Food, and You

The Partial Answer to Some of Your Mood Changes

Chapter 6.

Keeping Your Thoughts in Perspective

Activities That Can Help You Keep Your Thoughts in Perspective

Chapter 7.

Final Thoughts

INTRODUCTION

I feel miserable about everything. I can't stop feeling hopeless, helpless and worthless. I no longer believe my life is worth living. My thoughts of despair have become the stalker I can't escape. I can't continue living like this. I want to end my life and be done with this.

Similar thoughts went through my mind in the fall of 1986 at a dormitory at Washington State University where I pursued a graduate degree. I was twenty-seven and for years and years I had attended individual psychotherapy, group therapy sessions and had read self-help books. For over four years, I had also taken 400 mg/day of Desyrel an antidepressant. Nothing worked. To make matters worse, my short-term memory was becoming significantly impaired by the high dosage of the antidepressant. My heart showed signs of arrhythmia and the psychiatrist that was treating me asked me to consider discontinuing my graduate work.

I was tired and I didn't know how else to end feeling like my mind was being crushed by thoughts of helplessness, hopelessness, and worthlessness that continued to hurt my sense of self-worth regardless of what I did. I'd been experiencing feelings of sadness for as long as I could remember. As a kid I was bullied, which caused me to feel emotionally vulnerable all the time.

As I attended high school, I started weekly therapy sessions because I always felt worthless. During the years that I was bullied, I developed a negative self-image and did not see myself as someone worthy of respect or love.

By the time I began college, I was experiencing symptoms of depression and my mood swings were remarkable. I would be upbeat one minute and crying my eyes out the next.

After I finished college and pursued my graduate degree, my depression became the stalker within. It didn't matter what I did, whether I took on new activities, challenges, met exciting people, attended group therapy or saw my psychotherapist, thoughts of despair, helplessness, hopelessness and worthlessness followed me everywhere. No matter how hard I tried to get rid of them, my self-defeating thoughts were slowly becoming the stalker who wanted to remind me that the best way out was death.

One night, I sat in my dorm room feeling extremely depressed after attempting suicide for the first time. As I sat there, I glanced at the picture of my family on the desk. They stared at me as if asking, why.

I looked down hoping to find the answer but I didn't have one. All I knew was, I didn't have the will to live any longer. When I looked at the picture again, they were still staring at me. This time, they seemed sad. I realized then how much my death would have devastated their lives, especially my mother. It would've brought haunting thoughts and guilt. Deep down, I knew they weren't responsible for my condition, but they would've felt fully responsible and would have thought I was blaming them.

That was when I finally realized how important it was for me to learn how to endure my feelings of despair. If any one was to endure those types of feelings that stalked me daily it was I and not my family or those who knew me. Many people offered to help me overcome my condition, but I wasn't receptive to them. I couldn't understand why.

However, the answer was within my belief system. I began to realize that as long as I believed that my situation was hopeless; no one would be able to help. It was like trying to learn to walk on a wire 10 feet off the ground. If people don't believe they can do it, it doesn't matter how many others believe in them. They never succeed.

Conversely, if someone believed that learning to walk across a wire 1,000 feet above the ground is something that they can definitely do, they would do it no matter what others thought.

I then realized that I had failed to control the thoughts

of despair. Being withdrawn was the only life I knew. I had allowed circumstance to control me. Depression had absolute control of my life.

As I continued dealing with my thoughts of suicide, however, images of many less fortunate people began to flash through my mind. Images of those with paraplegia or quadriplegia, people stricken with crippling diseases, people that had lost their limbs to accidents and that were just happy to be alive. To be alive for them was a celebration.

As those images flashed through my mind, however, I realized that there was something really ironic about the way I lived my life. I could walk or run, make money at my own will or change my lifestyle, but I was ready to give up when I felt I couldn't endure my feelings of despair anymore. I began to wonder what kept me from overcoming my emotions.

It didn't take me long to figure it out. Those who were physically challenged entertained positive thoughts because they had a stronger belief system. They believed that being alive and experiencing even the simplest things in life was a celebration. As long as they lived nothing could stop them from a fruitful future. All they needed to do was stay alive and they would accomplish their goals.

Thoughts can have extraordinary power. Every major achievement mankind accomplished came about a thought. Mahatma Gandhi and Dr. Martin Luther King Jr., began their journeys to change their people's lives as the result of a thought they decided to pursue. The holocaust is an example of how a thought can lead to the brutal destruction of innocent lives. Thoughts are also the driving force of our lives. Those who think joyful thoughts experience joy. Those who think sad ones experience sadness.

Given that thoughts drive our lives and have the power to move masses to create or destroy, how could I control thoughts that turned against me and destroyed my self-esteem and will to live? I realized that I needed to find a way to separate my belief system, the source of my relentless feelings and thoughts of despair, from my real world because not a second would go by without me feeling, desponded. To that end I made the decision to name my belief system, the stalker within.

This would be different from those who hear voices and experience paranoia/schizophrenia. I did not hear voices nor felt paranoid. I only experienced feelings and thoughts of despair and hopelessness in a relentless manner.

This book is not intended to replace psychotherapy or medication. Instead, it was written to compliment them, to help change the self-destructive thoughts by modifying the belief system of those who have clinical depression. That aspect of clinical depression has been vastly ignored in most books written about the disease.

It is a well-known fact that antidepressants alone are not able to eliminate clinical depression. I feel strongly that if I had been able to focus on my belief system and kept my thoughts in perspective, when dealing with clinical depression, they wouldn't have threatened my life.

The formula for fighting self-defeating thoughts isn't directly named in this book. It works better when discovered by those who seek it. Once they do, they learn the power of awareness when dealing with thoughts of misery, failures, defeat, or guilt. Such thoughts promote confusion and are often responsible for making us feel as if our personal limitations were the true indicators of our potential as human beings.

The approach described here isn't to be used by those who hope to get rid of such thoughts. Only those who believe they can will be able to use it. People can't overcome limitations until they modify their belief system and truly believe they can. Believing you are ready to modify your belief system is to understand that no more effort is required to change your state of mind than to change self-destructive thoughts into ones that are simple, understanding and appreciative.

When reading, keep in mind that optimism and

pessimism is a state of mind that may be induced by affirmation or by sending repeated instructions to the subconscious through autosuggestion. By following the ideas in this book, you may convince your subconscious you're ready to entertain positive thoughts.

Always remember that simply reading over the words doesn't help. Unemotional words don't influence the subconscious. Inspiration to action is needed to break the mind free of being self-bound. I use self-bound to mean the times when people know what to do and still refuse to make any changes for the better.

Use this book to search for the answers that are useful in controlling your emotions and thoughts. This book isn't intended to give you the answers to your problems. The quest for answers is what gives purpose to people's existence. When people no longer care to answer questions, people face the void that can also lead to clinical depression and suicide.

Chapter 1

Keeping Your Mind Simple When Facing Clinical Depression

How I Developed a Simple Mind through Awareness

Comedian/entertainer Bill Cosby once said, "I do not know what the key to success is but the key to failure is to try to please all of the people all of the time." Up until the day of my suicide attempt, it is precisely what I had done. I had lived my life trying to please everyone.

My belief system was full of complexities that I could not understand or justify. Up until that day my goal in life had been to live up to everyone's expectations. I had never formulated my own ideals and had never defined myself. Goals had never been about me. They had been about what everybody else expected of me. I measured my success not by how many goals I had achieved but by how often I had met someone else's expectation.

The problem with this is that by trying to satisfy what everyone expected of me, I always felt overwhelmed and emotionally exhausted. And whenever I felt that I had not lived up to someone's expectations, I felt like I had suffered a crushing defeat rather than a setback. And the irony is that whenever I met someone's expectation I did not feel excited for myself. I felt excited for proving them right and not letting them down. As such my joys were short lived because the more I proved my peers right the bigger the expectations my peers had for things that I did not really care about.

Following my suicide attempt I began to realize that I needed to focus in modifying my belief system by developing and nurturing a simpler mind. However, to do that I had to become aware of whom I really was and get to know myself. A simple mind is one where you take care of yourself and no longer allow subconscious negative thoughts to stalk your mind. To have a simple mind is to make your existence a priority. What you have or don't have is not important. What you could have been or never were is not important. The horrible things that may have happened to you are not who you are. What it is important is the human being in you. The one who must make mistakes to learn because after all this is how human beings emotionally grow.

You must be able to feel and enjoy being you without letting your peers or thoughts that stalk your mind interfere with the human being that you are in this very moment. Again, you need to appreciate yourself for who you are right now and not for what you could have been or never were or what other people say you should have been but never were, or the horrible things that may have happened to you that shouldn't have happened.

It is also important not to allow your mind to be confused about who you are. I realized then that one of the most important steps to take when dealing with depression is to learn to understand the magnitude of one's confusion. With that, we can assess the scope of our limitations and can begin to develop a simple mind where you can just be yourself and not feel guilty.

With a confused mind, where life's priorities are unclear it's like having a cluttered storage room where you can't decide what things to get rid of. In the mind, this state gives us no idea of which goals or thoughts to let go or pursue. Meanwhile, hours or years pass, and our lives become lost in the universe of uncertainty.

A confused mind is easily overwhelmed. It can go through a paradise of experiences without feeling them. Moreover, it doesn't distinguish between the objective and subjective and is affected by all thoughts and events. It becomes easily saturated over emotional issues making it feel anger with itself and, possibly, saying or doing things later regretted.

Conversely, a simple mind goes through paradise feeling the experiences. You can even define your paradise as the ability to experience your life as it unfolds whether good or bad or even being one notch above rock bottom, which you can then use to build upon it. It is a paradise because there is nothing else important and exciting in your life other than experiencing that unique moment of accomplishment. After all, human beings are the only ones in this entire world that can experience and live through such emotions.

A simple mind also has a clear understanding about the meaning of unpleasant experiences and their importance, but it doesn't cling or become attached to any one experience, pleasant or unpleasant, because it knows that, in order to fully appreciate them, it ought to treat them as unique events. In essence, the simple mind is well focused and goal oriented. It can set priorities and doesn't let external forces change its direction.

This doesn't mean that the simple mind can only take on one responsibility at a time. A mind becomes simple only when it practices awareness, which can handle a multiplicity of things. That's the main difference between the simple and confused mind.

Awareness is achieved through understanding. The confused mind lacks that and is unclear about its priorities. The simple mind understands the scope of its ability to deal with the multiplicity of the external environment and is clear in its objective and purpose. That's why the simple mind isn't affected by past, present or future. Instead of thinking about what it should've or could've been, it simply is.

When we release self-defeating thoughts, guilt, anger, and the idea that the past is represented in the present, or when feelings of worthlessness and hopelessness that stalk our mind are finally restrained we can feel confident that we have developed a simple mind. After all, our ability to develop a simple mind is dependent on how much we understand and accept the past the present and the future.

A Life Gone Out of Order

It is not difficult to realize when you begin to lose focus. What is difficult is becoming aware of the consequence of such a state of mind. You slowly notice that your life is no longer in order. You begin to realize that you no longer have the grasp that you had in life. You may slowly become aware that your belief system is deeply conflicted.

Sitting in your apartment, where as a result of the depressing thoughts that stalk your mind, you may begin to feel that you lost your sense of direction. Your energy level is so low you couldn't follow through on your obligations and responsibilities.

Under those circumstances, your thoughts may only reflect your confused mind. Because of that, you might not be aware of the difficulties and consequences of such a lifestyle. Bill collectors start coming to your door, because their invoices were misplaced. You look for a clean shirt to wear, but there aren't any.

The lack of motivation has additional consequences. You begin to feel isolated and destitute. The worst part is that you'll fail to realize that it takes more energy and effort to deal with things like a job loss than to keep it.

Similarly, you don't realize it's easier to follow through on an appointment than to skip it or that life is easier when you try to be successful than when you decide to give up and fail.

Even though it takes too much effort to focus on your responsibilities when feeling depressed, it's important to take measures to become aware of the consequences of the way you live. You must take action to keep a conflicted belief system from running your life. Losing a job, because you didn't fulfill your responsibilities, has far-reaching consequences. If you can't pay the rent, your problems multiply. You might end up living on the streets.

By then you probably pushed away your friends too.

You'll feel the world is against you, although you turned against it.

Since you have a deeply conflicted belief system, not knowing how to control the negative thoughts that stalk you is the real problem. How difficult would it be to turn your life around and become the kind of person everyone count on? Who would seem to have it all together and would provide a sense of security for others. Doing that isn't as difficult as it would be to convince yourself that living a life where you don't care about your obligations and responsibilities is more complicated to live than one that's structured and satisfied for being able to let go of your troubling thoughts.

Keeping Life in Order

Not caring about obligations and responsibilities because of your conflicted belief system brings rejection and negative feelings. It is as if you are subconsciously seeking rejection because you feel that everything you believed is now in question. However, caring about your obligations and responsibilities brings acceptance and reward despite of how you feel about your life. Through my own experience with depression, I know that when we lose our motivation to succeed or appreciate things in life, we don't want to be rewarded or accepted.

However, if we want to overcome depression it's important that we give positive meaning to simple things and accept the rewards and acceptance by others. Be aware that if you don't your feelings of helplessness, hopelessness and worthlessness will only continue to destroy your self-esteem and self-worth. If you don't want those feelings controlling your life, don't let the rest of your life go out of order.

If there is a part of your life that doesn't satisfy you fully, it's important that you don't subconsciously use that as an excuse to let the rest of your life become out of order. If that happens, you'll have even more reason to justify your negative feelings, and your life will become even more uncertain and difficult.

This doesn't mean, of course, that maintaining a life in the face of depression is easy. It only means that if you are serious about regaining control of your life, you must have some degree of satisfaction, happiness and stability. That enables you to control your feelings and the negative thoughts that come with them.

Once you keep the rest of your life in order, you can move to the next step--- learning to let go of your self-defeating thoughts by carefully filtering them especially when you are expecting something bad to happen that could get you in a situation that you do not really want to be in. To filter your thoughts you must put your thoughts in perspective. To do that I put together an exercise that helped me achieve that. The exercise works better if you do not know its objective beforehand. However, during my desperate struggle with depression I felt the need to be sincere and objective with myself because I wanted to have a better understanding of my feelings. As such, I did this exercise that you can just read through and understand the point that I am trying to make or you can challenge yourself to be sincere and experience what I experienced when I did it. The exercise consists of considering alternative options for your current state of mind. On your first option you think about all the negative and destructive thoughts that are stalking your mind and that are making you feel that the worse possible outcome is imminent and you have no way out. Think also about how that scenario looks like.

On the second option think the least likely of the positive outcomes that in your mind have no chance of happening because it would be too good to be true. On the third option think about how a person who you look up to, would deal with your situation. Choose a positive person that you know and respect, an acquaintance that you admire, or a famous person that you have never met but whose personality you have admired because he or she has achieved unremarkable success. List the things that he or she would do and describe how you think they would deal with your situation if they were in your shoes. On the fourth option list the best possible outcome that you could achieve if your state of mind was strong and positive. The kind of person that you wish you could be.

After you are done, think about why the things that you thought about on option one need to happen. After all, if you have three other options that do not agree with your first one why should it happen? However, like I said if you decide to do this exercise you must be honest with yourself and not think about negative approaches to prove to yourself that your situation is truly hopeless. By being honest, you will begin to see your patterns, desires, and ego drives and you'll begin to understand how you can begin to change a belief system that produce negative thoughts and stalk your mind.

As you continue that process you'll understand the emptiness and impermanence of those patterns. As such, it becomes easier to abandon them, and you won't even have to try, because they slowly wither. When the light of awareness shines on thoughts, that lack substance, it diminishes the false and encourages the true.

When you achieve that, you'll experience a sense of satisfaction and peace. Transforming your thoughts doesn't mean you will have a trouble-free life. Your problems will still be there, but you'll have a growing sense of sanity and understanding of your situation.

It can't be done overnight. It's a discipline that needs to be developed over time. To be committed to overcome depression means working to improve that part of your life that is unfulfilling and drains you while simultaneously fighting to maintain the order in the rest of your life. Is that easy? No. But it's possible.

If you begin to view depression as an individual entity that has all the intentions to destroy your life, you will fight to keep it at bay. That's the only way to prevent depression from taking over your life. For if despite of your lack of energy, motivation and focus you manage to follow through with your obligations and commitments, you will have the satisfaction that you and not that entity is the one that controls your life.

Although you may not feel good about that at the

time, it'll prevent your negative feelings from taking over your life. In depression, preventing such feelings from taking over your thoughts is a major achievement.

To accomplish that you will need patience, persistence, courage, resilience, and determination. In my situation, I had to isolate myself from everything I felt had a negative influence on my thoughts and reminded me that my belief system was conflicted. I decided that, the self-defeating feelings that I experienced were not real. They were just a reaction to a flawed belief system that I had relied on for years but needed to change. I needed to stay away from such thoughts because like a real life stalker, they had no real purpose but could destroy me.

I surrounded myself with positive influences. I stopped watching any movies on TV or theatre that ended in tragedy or despair. I avoided people who made me feel uncomfortable or negative. I watched comedies and success stories and listened to music that inspired positive thoughts. I spent as little time alone in my apartment as I could. I limited my reading to news articles or books that inspired me.

I also visited places where people go to relax or have fun often just to watch them go about their lives. I would search for people that looked like they were at peace or happy. I would then ask myself what prevented me from being that way. Sometimes I would describe those reasons in a piece of paper. After I finished writing I would wait an hour or two or a full day to read what I wrote. I did this to get a fresh perspective of how my feelings changed about my reasons for not feeling at peace or happy. I noticed that my reasons changed over time. If I was thinking more positively at a later time, I would find that some of the reasons that I had written felt like nonsense. If I was feeling disheartened, I would find even more reasons not to be happy. That analysis made me realize that there was no real reason for me to feel less happy than others. If there had been a good reason (one that would be based on facts and not just feelings and perceptions) my thoughts and feelings would not have changed over time. I also was aware that the reason other people seemed at peace or happy wasn't because they never had experienced any tragedies or challenging circumstances.

If you disagree with this last statement, I challenge you to read about some of the best success stories in our generation. I found that the more challenges and tragedies they had faced in life the stronger their personality and the stronger their success was. I personally continue to feed on those types of stories. More recently I read the story of Lisa Williams, who at age 7 almost died after being raped and physically abused. After she graduated from high school she occasionally sold her body, when she did not have a job, so that she could eat. However, she then made the decision to finish college while living out of her car and working two jobs.

She then chose to earn her masters degree and eventually became a petroleum engineer. In August 2006 she became the founder of Living Water for Girls, a program that helps sexually exploited children across the U.S. start over. Today she is a pillar in her community and is the kind of person that if you came across would probably look at peace and confident not because she never faced challenges and tragedies but because she faced many hardships. She just turned those hardships into the building blocks for a stronger belief system that gave her the foundation to succeed beyond anyone's expectation.

As such, it is somewhat naive for anyone to think that a person may seem happy, peaceful, or confident because they never experienced difficult times in their lives or that somehow your hardships are harder than anyone else ever had. It is very important to put that in perspective when working to eliminate your negative thoughts and change your belief system. If you cling to the believe that no one had a worse life than yours that is fine but then challenge yourself to show that you can be a bigger success story than those who, in your view, experienced lesser hardships than you and succeeded. Nothing should hold you back. Only your mind can do that.

From my perspective, I began to realize that what limited me was that I always tried to reject who and what I was because my belief system was not based on my own convictions but those of my peers. That was what kept me from becoming a more peaceful and happy person. I concluded, through my own reading and observations, that the people that looked happy and at peace accepted themselves for who and what they were before they went on to become successful.

I also realized that one way to accomplish that was to enjoy myself whenever I was alone. I needed to go everywhere by myself and do my best to enjoy myself. I figured that if I could do that at whichever places I went, it would mean that I was becoming successful at changing that part of my belief system that dictated that to look normal I needed to be gregarious and be accompanied by people everywhere I went. I also realized that, when I began to do that with ease, people at the gatherings showed interest in meeting me. In essence, I realized that my depression was rooted in a belief system that produced thoughts of self-rejection.

That doesn't mean that you must learn to ignore your feelings or symptoms of depression. I couldn't do that. The best I could do was work around them. I got up in the morning and immediately felt hopeless. However, it was more productive to welcome and thank such thoughts, then treat them like a stalker who refused to leave. I knew the thoughts were there but I would not let them control my day. I was aware that changing some parts of my belief system or the stalker within would take time and work.

As such, it's important in such a situation not to let the mind dwell on negative thoughts but to question their objective. I had to evaluate what my negative thoughts would accomplish for me that day.

It's important to do your best to go about your daily routine as consistently as possible. If you have a major activity scheduled that day, and do not look forward to it, take a long walk beforehand and commit yourself to go to that activity. The walk will give you a rested outlook and will make your interactions at the event easier.

Walking is one of the best ways to distract your mind from self-defeating and depressing thoughts, because it becomes aware of its surroundings and can't focus on troubling issues as well. That gives a refreshing insight into your thoughts.

If you play chess, you know how valuable distracting your mind can be. When you plan your next move, and you find yourself trapped without a good one, it's more productive to walk for a minute and come back to the game.

When you do, you'll come back and see more options than you thought. Life is like a chess game--- you can't just dwell on one move. It's important to let go of present thoughts and deal with them later with a refreshed mind.

When we work around our troubling issues, it's important to be aware of the fact that everyone wants happiness; everyone struggles to fulfill desires, and fights mental or physical pain. However, if you learn in your heart and not just your mind that a life of joy doesn't mean seeking happiness, but being who you are, not to fulfill personal desires but to fulfill the needs of life, not to avoid pain but to live with it when necessary, you can eventually achieve true joy and fulfillment.

Letting Go

To let go is to be able to renounce whatever is going on in our thoughts and emotions that interfere with who we are and what we want even though our belief system may refuse to accept it. It's a way of being detached from the activities of the mind. Whenever we have an idea of how things are supposed to be or how we or others are supposed to be we're attached.

Such attachments can hamper our spiritual life. When they dominate us, they tend to create disharmony in our lives. In essence, if a real life stalker were to go away but your thoughts and emotions were still attached to his existence it will not make a difference whether or not the stalker went away because your emotions will continue to hurt you as if he was there. However, if you keep those thoughts from dominating your mind, such emotions are harmless.

The first step in letting go is to acknowledge that we're attached to an event, person, or thought and that they are part of a belief system that we may no longer need to accept. We tend to become attached to things that touch our lives. We cling to them, cherish them, and believe we're nothing without them.

"If I lose her, I'll die." "If the situation doesn't go my way, I'll kill myself."

When we require life to be as we expect, we suffer. Life can only be itself and doesn't follow a script. We must understand that.

For this reason it's important to learn to accept life as it is and to identify the attachments that dominate our feelings. Then we can study their true nature and discover they are impermanent and empty. With that awareness, we'll be able to understand that as thoughts, they can be absent if we choose. If we see our attachments as thoughts, we can let go of them without effort.

The second step in learning to let go is to identify our real problems. By definition, a problem is a question proposed for a solution. A situation that has no solution is considered a fact or an event and not a problem. The real problem is the kind of thoughts we associate with our disappointments or failures.

Losing a job isn't a real problem, because the problem is the thought we associate with that loss. If you feel that by losing your job your life will end, you'll have a problem. There is a solution---you can modify your thoughts and begin looking at it as a new beginning and submit job applications until you find another job and your problem will disappear.

If we feel that by losing our loved ones, we've lost ourselves, then we have a problem because it has a solution, which is that we're lost only as long as our belief system decides to entertain that thought.

Problems come from the definition that we give to our thoughts, which represent personal viewpoints ingrained in our belief system. More often than not, those thoughts are emotionally charged, too. It's important to remember that we can only let go of them if we clearly identify and understand the thought associated with a situation and the benefits/perils of holding onto it.

The third step in learning how to let go is to accept that right or wrong are only thoughts, too. It's not wrong to die, neither is it wrong to kill---as long as the thoughts associated with the actions justify them. Killing a soldier can be either right or wrong depending on if he's a friend or foe. Every time right and wrong are judged as such, the thoughts are impermanent and subjective.

They are impermanent, because an action or situation is considered wrong only when thoughts classify it that way. When the forces that entertain those thoughts disappear, so does the wrongfulness of the action or situation. They are subjective, because right and wrong are based on personal viewpoints rooted in our belief system.

It took me years for me to figure out how to let go of my self-defeating beliefs. However, once I did I became at peace with myself.

CHAPTER 2

Modifying Your Beliefs and Thoughts

Productive Self-talk and Our Quality of Life

After struggling with depression for years, one of the things that became apparent to me was that as a chronically depressed, I consistently reinforced self-destructive thoughts and beliefs. Every time something went wrong or someone was critical of me, I would worry, blame myself, and justify other people's negative judgments about me.

Along with those emotions, I also associated thoughts that made me feel worthless, incompetent and ignorant. Such a reaction was an automatic response that turned off objective thoughts.

Patterns for responding to uncomfortable situations in life are usually created early in life. That's one reason why different people approach uncomfortable situations differently. A situation that's uncomfortable for one person may not be uncomfortable to another because their belief systems differ.

Attending a gathering can be uncomfortable to some, while it's exciting to others. Living alone might feel uncomfortable and depressing to some and relaxing to others. It depends on how our belief systems were shaped as we grew up and got older.

If your peers were very critical of people who aren't gregarious, chances are you'll incorporate that type of criticism into your belief system and will react accordingly when you find it difficult to make friends. If your peers are critical of people who live alone, you'll feel a lot of discomfort if you have trouble finding someone to live with.

Such a pattern can be experienced in almost any situation in life. Unfortunately, in the midst of the confusion we fail to become aware of the fact that those feelings are the result of thoughts rooted in our belief system. They are a reflection of the belief system that we built based on either our own convictions or that of our peers.

It's important to remember that the same way we fail to question such thoughts and choose not to fight them we could change how we feel about them by changing the meaning we associate with those thoughts.

To avoid reinforcing destructive beliefs and thoughts while depressed and to change our feelings about a situation, it helps for us to become aware of who we are and what we like. Many times we go through our lives making decisions and judgments and do not pause to listen to our hearts.

When I was a teenager, my peers led me to believe that in order to be considered a normal person; I had to be gregarious and entertaining. I did none of that and as such I began to feel less than normal. Since I began to lack confidence I was many times bullied. I accepted that as my punishment for not meeting that criterion of "normal." However, I knew deep in my heart that I did not have any interest in being any of those things.

Nonetheless, I never paused to question the belief system that my peers defined for me and, thus, I never fought back. I in fact believed that I deserved to be bullied for not meeting the criteria that my peers had set out for me. Moreover, I never felt angry at the bullies and instead hoped that someday they would accept me and welcome me as a friend. Interestingly, if someone had asked me back then whether I felt angry about the bullies I would have said yes. However, if that had been true, I would have stood up for myself and fought back regardless of the consequences. Instead, I did none of that. I took it all in and deep in my heart I blamed and hated myself for it.

As such, every time I attended a high school gathering I felt uncomfortable. I knew what it was expected of me and I also knew I couldn't do it. My demeanor became one of fear, discomfort and tension. As a result I turned off anyone that met me and the bullies loved it because they knew that as long as I was alone and worried and felt sorry for myself, I would not fight back.

That reinforced my low self-esteem. I later understood that the reason I had such trouble at gatherings was because I reinforced my belief system with thoughts that I had to be gregarious like my peers. If I couldn't mingle well at gatherings, I didn't belong and I was not normal. What I failed to do was understand that those views were only thoughts produced by my belief system.

However, it is important to know that when we try to understand who we are, we have to instruct our mind to study itself. The very thing we are studying has to become the means or tool for studying it. Thus, at first we don't know how to approach the problem. All we know is that something doesn't feel right. In my situation, I continued going to gatherings and functions despite the fact that I felt uncomfortable at them. However, when we become aware that something like this does not feel right, we need to search for answers so that we can better understand how we need to modify our belief system. We need to filter our thoughts. By filtering my thoughts I finally understood why I did that. For me fun was watching other people having a good time.

I eventually concentrated on watching people have fun and go about their lives without worrying what others might think. Along with that, I began to understand that in terms of socializing, I just needed to engage in one on one interaction to feel good about myself.

After I began to define who I was and understood what was meaningful to me, I realized that to fully enjoy my life things would be simple. It's easier to watch people having fun than making fun ---- it's easier to engage one person in a conversation and not be the center of attention.

Once I felt comfortable about my decision I was soon able to go to gatherings and functions by myself feeling confident and relaxed. Not long after that I began to be approached by people who wanted to chat with me. As such, I was no longer that awkward person that no one cared to get to know. All I had to do was modify my belief system.

However, when dealing with depression, it's important not to train ourselves to just do positive thinking while at the same time ignoring our depressing feelings. If you did, you'd ignore the obvious, like trying to ignore a stalker who's staring at you. In my experience, it's a big challenge to stop feeling uncomfortable or depressed just by thinking positively.

It's more productive to filter your thoughts and exercise awareness so you can develop a simple mind and achieve understanding. If you understand how the stalker's mind works, what motivates him and what discourages him, you could live in peace, because you'd be in control of the situation. Similarly, by understanding stalking thoughts, you can learn to control them and improve your quality of life.

Our Culture and Our Quality of Life

Our culture plays a significant role on how we shape our beliefs. Towards the end of this section, I describe my views on some controversial issues. As you read my opinions, you may go through a range of emotions—disappointment, anger, sadness, frustration, gladness. Many of the things that I will say might make you disappointed or you may feel pleased.

Remember that those emotions don't come from my statements. Instead, they come from the thoughts or experiences you have associated with the events that I describe. You'll react according to the belief system you developed as you grew up.

This should give you a better perspective on how feelings of depression can be kept under control. The key to controlling your feelings lies within your ability to become aware of the fact that depression comes about the thoughts and feelings or emotions associated with unfavorable events. Some experts call this process, neuro-linguistic programming also known as neuro-associate conditioning. Neuro-linguistic programming can take place subconsciously while we are growing up and develop our belief system. However, techniques have now been developed where neuro-linguistic programming can also help you change your perceptions and emotions for the better. Such concepts were first described by Richard Bandler and John Grinder in 1975.

As such, read over this section and at the end of this chapter choose one of the viewpoints with which you disagree. Once you do, close your eyes and think that people, who agree with you, on possibly a very emotional issue, are in the minority. As you try to convince a very reluctant majority to agree with you, imagine what it would be to begin to feel hopeless because the majority fails to agree with you. As your optimism dwindles, you become aware of your heart rate, respiration rate, and the tension in your muscles. Once you do that, become aware that you're only entertaining thoughts. Your emotions will continue as long as you keep those thoughts in mind.

The more you disagree with my statements the stronger your emotions may become. Hopefully you may realize that in depression, similar dynamics may occur. Some of the issues I have described are controversial issues because I am hoping that you will find yourself strongly disagreeing with me on at least one of them. At that point it will be important for you to stop to filter your thoughts by analyzing and finding out how such emotions came about. Go back several years or go back to your childhood and try to remember the events that occurred that incorporated those emotions into your belief system. This process may also work with issues you may agree with but works better with the ones that you have strong emotions about, which usually come about the issues you disagree with.

Some of the views that I describe here came about changes that I made to my belief system. I had entirely opposite views before I began to change some of them. You may feel that my belief system changed for the worse. If that is the case, I encourage you to do the exercise at the end of this chapter.

It's important to understand how our belief system affects our feelings. We often train ourselves to absorb what our peers say without questioning it. When we begin to feel depressed about a specific situation, it's worthwhile to try to understand it and if necessary, reevaluate our belief system.

For example, we learn early in life that we shouldn't brag about ourselves. Humility seems to begin with the denial of our strengths. We seldom tell ourselves, *I'm good. I'm smart, I'm great, and I'm the best.* Our society usually does not reward us for that.

Society's often unspoken message is that people will help you and pay more attention to you when you have low self-esteem. Some people will more likely reward you more for developing negative emotions than positive ones. Only those who break away from those patterns and don't seek to be rewarded by others, but only to reward themselves, seem to have an easier time of succeeding. On many occasions, when we prefer to be rewarded by others, by getting their attention, it becomes natural for us to think about our negative qualities and to reinforce our negative emotions. Such cues show in our speech, demeanor, or when we face an uncomfortable situation, because we're hoping to be rewarded with attention.

When we choose to live that way, we tend to make statements about ourselves that are degrading or destructive. We also experience feelings of incompetence when things don't go our way. Unfortunately, these statements or feelings are linked to other feelings that can trigger a sense of hopelessness and the urge for self-punishment. Then we begin to feel like losers bound to be viewed as such forever.

However, those patterns are often associated with feelings and thoughts we developed early in life through our belief system. This is when the negative neuro-associate conditioning will kick in. It's possible that, as a child, you did something wrong or didn't accomplish a task. As a result, you may have felt physically or emotionally rejected by your family or peers. As such, as a youngster or adult, you'll experience those same feelings again and will probably feel the need to punish yourself. You'll experience low self-esteem every time you do something wrong, when someone corrects you for not doing a job well, or when you fail at something. You will experience those emotions all over again just like you did when you were a child and were scolded for doing something wrong.

People don't need to have been physically abused to feel less than human when someone disapproves of them. It all depends on how emotionally susceptible you were to acts of rejection or disapproval when you grew up and how often they happened. My parents didn't realize that every time they expressed their dissatisfaction towards me, it carved away at my sense of self-worth. The reason for that was my lack of emotional strength. Some of us have an emotional makeup that is softer than that of other people who are able to tolerate strong punishment.

Nevertheless, all that began to change as soon as I changed my beliefs and thoughts about myself and how I wanted to live.

Although it's true that beliefs and thoughts define who we are, it's important to be aware that when we focus on our beliefs, we're actually not focusing on ourselves. We're in fact focusing on events experienced earlier in life and the people who shaped our belief system.

That's especially true when we experience low self-esteem and are depressed. If we're unaware of the pattern, then whenever we take action, make a decision, or seek to resolve our feelings, we run the risk of making hurtful decisions.

We may decide to conform to past events and judgments, where we reach a decision based on false assumptions. Our decisions are often made in an effort to prove our peers or loved ones right or wrong. If we love them dearly, we believe there is no need to prove them wrong. If we don't, we try to avoid proving them right.

If you were told that you aren't smart enough to get through college, you may choose not to apply to college and avoid proving your peers right. Similarly, if you totally trust what your loved ones say, you may decide not to waste your time challenging their judgment. You believe they know more than you do about your potential.

As such, if you enrolled in college anyway, you'd probably go in already defeated and with great self-doubt that would suck a lot of energy out of your will power. You wouldn't give 100% of your effort and might fail your courses, then drop out as your loved ones predicted. In that case you'd be acting according to your belief system, which conforms to other people's expectations, not your own potential.

Only when you take control of your life will you be able to focus on feelings that address your potential and open the door to new opportunities and not your conflicted belief system. If you focus on such feelings, you can take the action you desire. You won't experience feelings of helplessness, hopelessness, and worthlessness if you achieved undesired results, because you're trying to reward yourself, not to prove anything to anyone.

In our society, beliefs are also the limiting factor of personal growth and performance. The unspoken message in our society about a person with paraplegia or quadriplegia, also rooted in a belief system, is that they're destined to live in a wheelchair. The ones with a stronger belief system that broke through such barriers became successful but the vast majority will never become part of the working class. I have yet to see a paraplegic become a virtuoso musician, the leader of a popular band, or a world famous writer of fiction books.

I would love to see a person with paraplegia become an acclaimed composer or a famous poet. Nothing should be allowed to stop us from becoming our best. The only limiting factor is our belief that physically challenged people that are wheelchair bound do not have much chance for success and how that is communicated to the physically challenged.

Wheelchairs seem designed with that in mind. There's not much flexibility in a wheelchair to do anything but propel a chair.

It's ironic to see how advanced our technology is and how it has failed to meet the needs of the physically challenged. We can adjust the Hubble telescope by sending signals from Earth, helping it remain productive, yet we can't help people remain productive once they're physically challenged or wheelchair bound.

So far, no one has designed wheelchairs that will serve as a workbench for the physically challenged. If that were done, physically challenged people would be able to learn new skills, play musical instruments, design computer programs, write songs or books, design advanced electronic devices, assemble equipment, knit quilts, or contribute to fashion design.

People can teach themselves to become an authority in any field just by reading available books. The tools the physically challenged need to succeed can be found anywhere. It's only a matter of changing the way we think about their limitations so that the physically challenged can also believe that success is within their reach.

As such, wheelchair bound people, have been limited to living in wheelchairs and nothing else. We'll never be able to see such changes unless our beliefs about their limitations change. Only when we entertain thoughts about the usefulness of a wheelchair instead of the disadvantages will we be able to become more creative in assisting the physically challenged become successful.

In the same way, children who've been victims of physical or sexual abuse struggle to become successful. If we were victims of such atrocities as children, we would struggle with the notion of whether we deserve to be respected as human beings. Our minds would be filled with feelings of worthlessness and self-pity.

Such a sense of worthlessness would be carved so deeply into our emotions that guilt could surface. Then there would be nothing but self-hate and deep emotional pain for years. We'd have to struggle with the belief that we could've done something to prevent the abuse, and we'd feel totally responsible for our misfortunes. It is a belief that can destroy anyone's sense of self-respect. However, it is important to realize that it is just a belief that we have chosen to accept as real. As such, we must do everything within our power to reject it because we do have that option.

The reason we may feel guilty is because of the unspoken message in our society that promote those feelings of guilt and self-pity. The message from our society often reinforces the belief that we are responsible for the bad things that happen to us. Another unspoken message from our society is that vulnerable kids from dysfunctional families don't deserve respect or that those who became victims of sexual abuse did something to bring that onto themselves. Young people who never found a permanent home in which to live often deal with the fact that they are classified by society as inferiors. That begins early in school, where their peers degrade and reject them for living in group homes or in foster care and for not having a real home.

Females are also more affected than males by society's convictions. Homeless girls who live alone, in group homes, or on the streets run a high risk of becoming victims of sexual assault and physical abuse. Some men tend to believe that girls on the streets won't prosecute their assailants or that they are promiscuous or prostitutes and not really victims.

We rarely see members of society taking responsibility for the fact that society is often responsible for such viewpoints and very little is done to change them.

Some years ago, a young woman was raped on a pool table at a bar while others stood around and cheered. They seemed to believe it was an acceptable thing, because she came to the bar freely. They interpreted her presence as consent.

Once a person becomes a victim of sexual or physical abuse or part of the foster-care system, they'll have good reasons to retain self-destructive, unhappy thoughts. Their thoughts will reflect what they've learned from their peers. That will continue to be the case until society sends the message that regardless of how anyone came into the world or where he or she grew up; they're as valuable as anyone else.

Such thoughts also play a role on how we as individuals judge other people's lives. In Florida, a man was acquitted from raping a woman, because the jury believed that because of the way she dressed she deserved to be raped. They said she asked for it by dressing up too provocatively.

In some third-world countries, women are treated as maids or slaves. In those cultures, that's a woman's role. That is the belief system that their societies promote. Along those same lines, according to beliefs in our society, it's OK for the wife to depend on her husband for income, but it's not OK for the man to depend on his wife's income.

Studies have shown that marriage isn't likely to last if the wife is highly educated, while the husband has no education. If the woman depends on her husband's income, she still has an honorable profession as a homemaker. If the man depends on his wife's income, he may be labeled by some a loser.

A married man can date and have sexual relations with another woman and the man's reputation is seldom affected unless it is debated in a public forum. Some consider him lucky or a man who knows how to get a woman's attention. Furthermore, his personal life is no one else's business unless he is a public role model.

If a married woman dates and has sexual relations with other men, she's likely to be called a slut or a whore, someone unworthy of respect. If she holds an executive position, she's more likely to lose her job than a man if there are rumors about her lifestyle. Contrary to men, her personal life is everyone's business.

If, at any point, she becomes victim of rape, it would be difficult for her to have the man prosecuted. By then, she would have a reputation that would make it difficult to separate rape from consent.

As a result, women are more emotionally affected than men when they deal with such situations because their thoughts come about the negative aspects society reinforces in their belief system.

Beliefs of our society also affect the lives of homosexuals. By taking a role other than what our society expected of them, they lose the right to be treated with the same respect straight people get. Many in our society believe that people choose to be homosexual by choice. That belief is utter nonsense because no one in his right mind would prefer to be homosexual given the deplorable consequences associated with being a homosexual or transsexual in our society.

The judicial system is another aspect of our society that is affected by beliefs, which can be clearly seen in the way the US Supreme Court works. There are nine judges in the Supreme Court, who are supposedly experts at interpreting law. Nevertheless, there is seldom unity in their views. They have equal access to resources to help them interpret a specific law, but their personal convictions often help them make their decisions. After all, they are all highly educated, highly proficient in interpreting the law. Their only difference is how their belief system was shaped through their lives.

When there are five of the nine judges who believe the ninth and fourteenth amendments of the constitution protect a woman's right to choose an abortion, then the law is enforced as such, and society abides by it. Some members of our society may protest but the issue is nonetheless protected by law. If twenty years later, the balance shifts, and five of the nine judges believe that the ninth and fourteenth amendments don't protect a woman's right to an abortion, then the law changes. Suddenly, the government moves to punish what had been protected by law.

Similar situations have occurred over flag burning,

school prayer, and civil rights. Depending on our belief system, we consider either side of those issues wrong or right.

Beliefs also play a key role on how successful society is at fighting drugs. When the sale of alcohol was illegal, many criminals profited from illegal activities, and many innocent people died from alcohol-related crimes. When the law changed, criminals lost their profits, and associated crimes virtually disappeared. Society decided to transform something that was socially unacceptable into something glamorous. Although many innocent people today die from alcohol-related incidents and health problems, alcohol is still acceptable. Those who lost their lives fighting the war against alcohol lost something very precious protecting a law that was based on a different belief system.

Similarly, society decided the best way to eliminate addiction to nicotine was to educate people about the dangers of smoking cigarettes, not by making it illegal. If it were made illegal, America would face a similar situation to the time when alcohol was illegal during the years of the prohibition. Criminals would once again profit, and innocent people would be victimized.

Ironically, society has decided that the best way to eliminate abuse of other substances is by making them illegal. Criminals, that could not otherwise afford to buy a trailer home, have made billions of dollars from the sale of such drugs and bought mansions. As a result, many innocent victims die every year when drug addicts kill them in order to steal money or goods to sell to support their habit.

Society would like to believe that the thousands of criminals who make all that money will stop selling drugs and be happy to become poor for fear of being put in jail or face the death penalty. Our culture chose to believe that the benefits of living poor or depending on welfare outweighs the risk of selling drugs and making billions of dollars. It refuses to accept the fact that many of those criminals sell drugs, because they believe it's better to be dead than poor.

As the risk of selling drugs increases, the profit for the big-time dealers rises. That helps them make enough money to hire assassins to kill innocent people who accidentally witness a sale. They also have ways to get around the legal system, which reduces their risk.

If society believed that if the use of those drugs was made legal, but the sale of them for a profit was not, then we'd have a system by which the government would provide the drugs for a fee. That would eliminate those who make enormous profits. Dealers would no longer be in public schools, recruiting children to push the drugs or as new customers. Teenage dealers would cease to exist because the profit motive would vanish. Innocent people would be spared, because addicts wouldn't have to attack them in order to get money for their habit. Crimes associated with the sale of illegal drugs in America would be reduced considerably.

The billions of dollars the government spends fighting drug abuse could be used to treat and educate those who have become addicted and to provide free health care to our children. It's unfortunate that such a realistic approach isn't possible until society changes its beliefs. The majority in our society doesn't realize that the drug dealers are the first that would be hurt by such a move and might be the ones to oppose it, because they would no longer be able to reap billions in profits.

In California where the sale of medical marijuana is allowed, the marijuana growers opposed making recreational marijuana legal because they said that when the sale of medical marijuana became legal, the profits they were making from the sale of marijuana plunged due to the competition and they couldn't afford to sell cheaper marijuana.

To date there is not a corner in this country where illegal drugs are not sold or people cannot use them if they chose to. Yet the major argument for making the drugs illegal is the belief many in our society have that if recreational drugs became legal many more people would use them. The reality is that it is hard to imagine how many more people would use illegal drugs. Illegal drugs are available anytime and everywhere in this country including our prison system where the laws are strictly enforced and prisoners are routinely monitored. They are more available than prescription drugs are. Unfortunately the drugs will remain illegal for as long as such belief system continues to be nurtured in our society.

Another example of how society's beliefs can trigger thoughts of depression has to do with the aspect of virginity. More than seventy years ago, it was degrading and unacceptable for a woman to lose her virginity before marriage.

Such women fought rejection, loneliness, and depression. Today, it's widely acceptable for an unmarried couple to live together. If the relationship doesn't work out, the woman has little problem moving to another one. Society doesn't believe that virginity is related to loyalty or a good marriage the way it did 70 years ago. Consequently, the loss of virginity rarely causes clinical depression to the extent that it did 70 years ago.

Nevertheless, to this day in our society the term slut or whore does not apply to men. Men with promiscuous behavior are given a more elite name like Casanova or Playboy. As such, some women may get depressed once their peers begin to spread rumors about their behavior with members of the opposite sex while men are not likely to feel depressed about what their peers might say about their promiscuous behavior. Some men may not feel thrilled about being known as a Casanova or a playboy but overall men won't experience depression for being part of such rumors especially if they are single. The important thing to remember is that it is the exact same behavior but it is judged differently by our peers because of the belief system that has prevailed in our society for many generations.

In short, it is the thought associated with our belief system that counts. The thoughts that we associate with what our peers call us will determine whether we get depressed about it or not. By staying away from negative thoughts we may avoid feeling depressed. We are in absolute control of that.

For this reason it's important that we recognize our feelings and beliefs and how they're influenced by the judgment exercised by our peers. Our success at overcoming depression will frequently depend on how we break from such beliefs and the people who reinforce them. If our individual controversial beliefs are shared by the majority of the population, they could become society's beliefs. Society would then create laws to guarantee the freedom to exercise those beliefs.

As society ages, the next generation might consider some of the previous beliefs impractical and unproductive, because they no longer satisfy people's needs. The transition from traditional beliefs into practical, realistic ones is sometimes violent. There are those who are willing to die for what they believe is right, and others who are willing to kill for what they believe is wrong. The outcome of such a transition lays the basis for society's problems. It defines the thoughts that give happiness or sadness in people's lives.

As such, when you struggle with depression, it's important to realize that those feelings may've come about because you responded to a specific event or situation out of false emotions that may have developed from beliefs that exist in our culture. When people respond out of false emotions, the thought associated with them usually carries memories from the past or worries about the future, which translates into anxiety.

Anxiety is the emotion that stretches between the real and unreal, the distance between the way things are and the way someone wishes they were. If people lose their optimism and hope, such thoughts feel like shattered dreams, and depression may ensue. We tend to experience depression when we feel we've lost our sense of direction and purpose.

That sense of direction may have come from what is reinforced in our culture. If you have to drop out of school due to circumstances that are beyond your control, you may feel lost because in our culture you are expected to get a degree in college if you want to become successful. Even though there are plenty of very successful people that have defied that logic, you nevertheless may feel obligated to meet society's expectation if your belief system dictates it.

Unfortunately, those shattered dreams can sometimes overwhelm us with negative emotions. We exclude any positive influence associated with the undesirable outcomes and then lose hope.

We turn to a fantasy of possibilities, where we entertain the thought that we don't have a chance for a good life. What we ought to realize is that in the most extreme circumstances, such suffering can be brought under control if we accept the fact that our disappointment is a thought defined by the mind that is rooted in our belief system. If an outcome feels unpleasant, we can choose to be at peace if we wish.

It's the journey, not the attainment of a pleasant outcome that makes the pursuit worthwhile. If for some reason you do not achieve the outcome that you desired you have reasons to celebrate the lessons that you learned through that journey instead of dwelling on what you didn't accomplish. However, whether you decide to celebrate that or not is really up to you. No one can do that for you. Only you can make that journey feel meaningful.

As I mentioned at the beginning of this chapter, if you were able to identify issues that you strongly disagree with, try to come up with a description of the type of environment or background that could have helped you think differently about these issues. The objective of this exercise is not to change your view on the issues but to help you realize that in depression similar dynamics occur.

In essence, you can choose to entertain thoughts that make you feel depressed or you can choose to find the roots of those emotions and change how you feel about them. If you want to change your emotions about a situation you can describe the environment that would allow you to experience positive emotions about the situation. You can then create a list of the things that you would need to do to permanently create that environment. After you do that, create a list of the things that a person you have a great deal of respect for, or that you admire, would do to create that environment. Reconcile his or her approach with yours. Describe the things that you cannot do the same way and list those barriers. Work to destroy at least one of those barriers.

Sometimes by destroying just one of those barriers you may find that many doors will open for you and that can change the dynamics of depression. Once I destroyed the barrier that made me feel uncomfortable when I went to gatherings, I felt more confident and relaxed regardless of where I went. People then began to approach me just to chat. As such, I became part of the crowd and that in turn allowed me to break other barriers.

Remember that to destroy that barrier all I had to do was change my belief system. If you cannot destroy one of those barriers on your own get some help. Read other self-help books that will complement this one, join a support group or work with a mental health professional. You can also volunteer to work for organizations that help destitute people. In my case I volunteered to work with organizations that helped runaway and homeless kids. That work further contributed to removing additional barriers and changing my belief system.

Restructuring Your Self-talk

Self destructive feelings can manifest in many ways. Some people may decide to drop out of school if they fail a class while in college. Others that get constructive criticism at work might feel so angered they quit. The ones that are fired from a job or fail an important test, might experience feelings of incompetence and stop pursuing worthwhile goals. Some might even entertain thoughts of suicide.

We can however, change this response by making statements to ourselves that are associated with feelings of understanding, comprehension, and awareness. If you want to test how statements affect your feelings, close your eyes and imagine someone asking you to act in a scene in which you're supposed to act like an insane person who wants to destroy things. If you repeat to yourself, "I am angry, I am angry." You will be able to feel anger.

If you say to yourself, "I am fascinating, I am fascinating," or "I am extraordinary, I am extraordinary," it would be difficult to entertain angry thoughts and express your anger. The reason is that the words *fascinating* and *extraordinary* aren't associated with feelings of destruction or distress. Instead, the mind tries to rationalize such statements. This is a typical example of neuro-linguistic programming. Throughout our lives we have made neuro-associations between the word angry and the angry feelings that we experience but had not done the same with the words fascinating and extraordinary.

As such, the brain interprets the word extraordinary as something out of the ordinary because of the neuro-associations that we have made through the years. Also, the word fascinating might be interpreted as interesting, unusual or unexpected. The mind will send a message of disbelief to the senses, and there won't be any anger. Again, this is another example of neuro-linguistic programming.

If you find yourself dealing with an uncomfortable situation you created, instead of saying self-defeating statements, you can say, "This is fascinating," or "This is extraordinary." That type of self-talk could help prevent self-destructive feelings which might trigger depression.

It's true that you might still experience feelings of frustration even if you talk to yourself this way. However, frustration does not need to be linked to self-destructive thoughts, which can happen when you choose to say self-defeating statements. If something went wrong, it was probably out of your control and, thus it can be fascinating. Those statements are useful in controlling anger as long as you believe them. You'll need to believe them with greater conviction than you have for self-defeating statements.

Let me give you an example, one Sunday, I was supposed to go to San Francisco for a conference in which I would speak the following afternoon. My plane was scheduled to leave Sunday at Seven-thirty in the evening. The previous week, I arranged for a cab to pick me up at six o'clock.

By six-thirty, the cab still hadn't come. I called and found out they made a mistake and were planning to pick me up at six o'clock in the morning.

It was seven 0'clock by the time I got a cab. Normally, it took twenty minutes to reach the airport, so I assumed I'd still make it. I reached the airport and ran in to read a monitor to see which gate I needed.

To my surprise, the monitor showed that my plane already departed. My ticket stated departure at seven-thirty. I went to the counter to demand an explanation and learned the flight had been rescheduled to leave fifteen minutes early.

Since feelings and thoughts that reinforced depression were always in my mind, I immediately began making statements to myself that were self-defeating.

I'm incompetent, I thought. *I've been traveling for years, and I still haven't learned how to avoid this nonsense. I should've reconfirmed my flight twelve hours before departure.*

I wanted to bang my head against the wall, because I could've also avoided the whole thing by checking with the cab company. Before I went too far with those thoughts, I realized I had the choice to see the situation from another perspective. There was good reason to be fascinated with the situation. Everything that could go wrong went wrong. So maybe things were meant to happen that way. Perhaps if I had done everything right the flight might have even been canceled. The way everything worked out to go simultaneously wrong was fascinating.

I had two choices for how to feel about my situation, I could feel self-hate and self-destruction for not being careful, or I could feel disbelief and fascination for how everything became coordinated to go wrong so that I would miss my flight. With the former, I proved once again I was irresponsible and unreliable. With the latter, I faced the fact that life is a collection of pleasant and unpleasant events that come from being a human being.

My only alternative was to book another flight. When I started looking at the situation from the perspective of disbelief, I felt more rational and was more productive the rest of the evening. The next flight would leave at six o'clock the following morning, which wouldn't affect my schedule, because the time difference between Detroit and San Francisco gave me the leeway I needed to arrive in time to attend all the sessions and still give my talk. Thus, I suddenly realized that not everything that could go wrong went wrong after all. I still came out ahead. I in fact had no need to waste my energy over something inconsequential.

If you want to restructure your feelings and beliefs, when you feel angry, use statements of understanding and self-appreciation. Start by acknowledging you're a human being, not God. You can't make everything go right all the time.

Begin to put together a list of positive statements when you find yourself feeling positive. Write the supportive statements that come to your mind on a card and neuro-associate those statements with the positive feelings that you are experiencing at that moment by closing your eyes and experiencing them. Sense your emotions of satisfaction and self-worth. Create statements according to the feelings and beliefs you need to restructure, and make sure you voice your feelings, not your qualities as a human being. Don't deny your feelings just redirect them toward something understandable, rational, and acceptable. It's not reasonable to make yourself believe you're happy when you're sad, or to say you succeeded when you failed. The purpose isn't to lie to yourself or to live in denial.

If you are emotionally in a rot, when attempting this exercise, you can still close your eyes and visualize a time when you felt either happy or relaxed. While you are doing that think about statements of support that you would make to someone you would like to help while you are relaxed. Feel the energy. Sense your emotions when you do that and describe those statements on a card. The next time that you have a bad experience, take out your card and read your statements while at the same time trying to sense the emotions you experienced when you wrote them.

You must use statements to describe your feelings, because qualifying statements about our personalities are the product of our beliefs. Those statements are usually linked to feelings that are rooted in our belief system, which can be self-defeating and destructive.

For example, if you were someone's secretary, and you forgot to give your boss a message about a rescheduled meeting, he might be angry at you for missing the meeting. You would reinforce your belief that you're irresponsible and incompetent if you said, "This is frustrating, I can't believe I was so irresponsible. I must be mentally challenged. I'll be lucky if he doesn't fire me because I really deserve that."

Instead if you said, "This is frustrating. I owe myself a break. I am human and because of that I will eat lunch or dinner at a place that makes me feel very relaxed. If you instead say, "This is frustrating I need to be more careful," the word "careful" describes a quality in you that could reinforce your low self-esteem if someone in your past hurt your feelings by calling you careless. Similarly, if your peers or your parents criticized you, saying you couldn't do anything right, you'd be reinforcing that belief. Then you'd experience the same feelings your peers or parents made you feel when you made a mistake. That could trigger the urge to punish yourself. You could in fact end up feeling bad about the incident for the rest of the day.

You may even experience a day where everything goes wrong. It's not necessary to tell yourself to be more careful. The fact that you felt frustrated about the incident is enough to remind you of that. You wouldn't be avoiding assuming responsibility for rewarding yourself with lunch either because in the back of your mind you already know it was bad. You just need to modify your neuro-associations to prevent self-defeating thoughts from taking over your day or week.

In short, keep things in perspective, because there's nothing to be gained by dwelling on things you can't change.

Restructuring Feelings of Guilt

When we struggle with depression, it's easy to dwell on situations considered undesirable. If we lose a loved one in a tragic accident, and we believe we could've prevented it somehow, we will feel guilt.

In the case of losing a child we might start thinking, "*I should not have let him go alone. If I hadn't he'd still be alive. I'm such a lousy parent.*"

We may also focus on the idea that we deserve to be miserable for life by thinking, "*I just want to die, I am a worthless piece of crap who couldn't predict what was going to happen. It was obvious and I didn't stop it.*"

If you analyze these statements carefully, there's a common denominator to all of them. They mostly focus on personal qualities that assume the blame for the undesirable outcome. If we explore the undercurrents of those statements, we find there is a lot of unexpressed anger. It's reasonable to think that the reason people put the blame on themselves is because they learned to feel responsible for everything that went wrong in their lives. Because of their belief system, they refuse to share the responsibility with the victim.

Such people sometimes act like superheroes, because they feel they're the only ones with the knowledge and ability to prevent all undesirable outcomes. They sometimes believe that the victim depended on them to make things come out right. Nothing could've happened by chance or just plain ignorance.

Thus, it would be more practical and productive to redirect guilt feelings and put them in a more realistic perspective. Although it's hard to admit, when people blame themselves for the loss of a loved one, their deep feelings are actually misdirected anger that the person feels toward the victim.

Such people would probably wish they could say, "I'm angry, because he left me and created such sadness in my life." "I'm angry because he died." Those statements also have a common denominator. They address a feeling, not personal qualities or beliefs. As a result, people don't need to entertain self-destructive thoughts. The need to entertain those types of thoughts sometimes comes from beliefs about low self-esteem, low self-worth, and low self-respect. The objective of this approach is not to avoid assuming responsibility for your actions, but to share them and be fair to yourself. It's not fair to assume you've got total control over incidents that are tragic or disappointing. No human being controls life or fate.

If people are realistic about their limitations, they learn to accept the fact that there are two choices--- to be unfair to oneself and assume all the blame, or to be realistic and admit that if they could stop all undesirable events, life would lose its purpose. Many times you need more than yourself to prevent a tragedy or a disappointing outcome.

The fact is that the true purpose of life is found in the challenges we face in making undesirable outcomes work for us. We need to understand that the journey in which we embark to prevent, and, if possible, modify undesirable outcomes gives purpose to our existence.

Would we feel good about ourselves if we could control life? How would we find any joy in it?

Joys come from the fact that even though we have no control over life, we can make things happen if we work hard at it. That's where the magic of enjoying our lives comes in.

If we keep in mind that we always have more than one choice for interpreting things, we can minimize the negative impact unfortunate events have in life. If a relationship doesn't work out, a person can both feel guilty and take all the blame, or he can be more objective and share it by accepting the fact that the other party wasn't willing to work things out. If he or she had, things would've been better.

What we have to keep in mind is that when something troubles us, we dwell on what could've or should've happened. We think hard, as if thinking was the answer to the problem. Only when we learn to experience our feelings, not the thoughts that continue to stalk our feelings, can we begin to heal.

If a three-year-old baby loses his mother in an accident, the baby doesn't dwell on its thoughts and has no concept of death. It reacts to its mother's absence and only feels that reality. Babies experience their feelings and resolve them by crying and expressing sadness. They don't resolve their feelings by allowing thoughts of guilt to stalk them about the loss.

Because of their brain function limitations, they don't project their thoughts to fantasies of how things could've turned out differently if only they'd acted another way. Babies deal with the moment and then release it. Adults that are emotionally soft could benefit from such abilities or the lack thereof. Adults sometimes choose to invest a lot of time and energy over possibilities that are impractical. If felt unchecked, such thoughts can lead to major depression.

It's important to remember that thoughts and emotions associated with guilt are impermanent. Guilt comes from disappointments, which are feelings based on thoughts produced by our belief system. Regardless of what we do to prevent disappointments, what we need to remember is that we're all protagonists of our own movie. Life is the producer and director. We don't control the plot. All we can do is contribute to it in real time. This is something we cannot rehearse for.

As such, the first step in dealing with feelings of guilt is to accept that reality and realize we're in the movie to serve, not to be served. At the end of a scene, we should be satisfied with our performance, because we did our best and life does not give us a chance to rehearse.

The second step is to accept that those thoughts associated with feelings of guilt have no reality and are empty. If we see them as real, they can create harm. We won't be able to abandon such thoughts until we stop entertaining them. It's important to look at such feelings as if we were watching a movie from the outside, not the inside. Only then can we put our thoughts in perspective and let things go.

That principle applies to all feelings of guilt regardless of their origin. The only reason I used a tragic event for an example was because they are powerful experiences that can trigger devastating feelings of depression. They're more complex to work with than other experiences.

Restructuring Feelings of Failure

As with feelings of guilt, a sense of failure is another feeling that predominates when we get depressed. Because of their belief system people sometimes view themselves as failures for not accomplishing a specific goal or for having undesirable outcomes while pursuing that goal. It's unfortunate that people view such outcomes as failures, not achievements. By doing that, they invalidate themselves for trying to achieve their goal.

Webster's dictionary defines failure as; *to fall short*, *to abandon*, *to stop operating*. Failure can be termed lack of action. Only when we stop taking action or abandon our effort to reach a goal have we failed. Until then, we are on our journey to accomplish our goal and our undesired outcomes should be considered steps towards the fulfillment of that goal.

If you fail a test because of the way it was designed, you can believe you were incompetent, or you can believe the teacher has an odd way of writing exams. Instead of getting angry about it, you can feel fascinated by the testing method. Then it's up to you to accept the challenge of finding another way to study for that teacher.

If you focus on the belief that you're incompetent, you're setting yourself up for a disappointment. That brings low self-esteem and lack of motivation, which, in turn prevents you from studying objectively for the next test. If you gave in to such thinking, you'd find a good reason to consider yourself a failure. As long as you strive to reach your goal, you're on a journey where every step or undesired outcome is an achievement, not a failure.

It's important to realize that it's unrealistic to expect to achieve our desired outcome with every action. The biggest success stories usually come from those who pursued their goals and found more undesirable outcomes than desirable ones. The number of undesirable outcomes from a specific action always outweighs the desirable ones. Sometimes, those odds are a million to one.

For example, scientists have tried for years to produce a molecular transporter. To date, after thousands of attempts, no one can tell if it will ever be done. Does that mean they should abandon their efforts?

Thomas Edison, one of the greatest inventors of the previous century, was in a similar situation when he tried to create the light bulb. The scientific community criticized him and labeled him a failure.

When a group of reporters brought that to his attention, he replied, "I haven't failed. I just discovered thousands of ways a light bulb won't work.

For that reason, when you feel depressed and feel a failure, it's important that you create a plan and follow it. Redefine your goals if the previous ones no longer interest you. Use your undesired outcomes to help design a new plan. You need a sense of direction in order to overcome feelings of depression.

There are many ways to create a plan of action. Your plan should be specific, not vague. Planning to get rich isn't a goal. You should define exactly what it is about being rich that excites you. Do you want to be your own boss? Do you want to own a house or car? Do you want to travel?

You must be specific. For some of those goals, you don't need to be financially rich to have what you wish. If you design a plan to budget the money that you need, you'll accomplish many if not all of your goals.

You could also be more specific. Perhaps you want a castle, not a house, and Ferrari, not just any car. Instead of travel, you'd like to own an airplane. In such cases, you must design a more ambitious plan and decide what kind of career you'd need to give you the necessary financial strength.

Decide how much money you'll need, the expertise and personnel required, and the resources necessary. Two best-selling books by George S. Clason and Napoleon Hill, The Richest Man in Babylon, and Think and Grow Rich, describe realistic ways to achieve such goals.

You can use that principle with every aspect of your life --- physical fitness, family, religion, mental health, relationships, or finance. Make your goals specific and outline them in detail. Include the sacrifices you need to make, like spending less time with family and friends. That way, you'll feel better about the sacrifices too.

Understanding Success

Many people believe that if they were financially wealthy, they'd no longer be depressed. Some people talk about success as if it were a fantasy or something only lucky, smart people achieve. Webster's defines success as a *favorable result*. Earl Nightingale, an inspiring speaker on personal growth, used to say that success is the progressive realization of a worthy ideal. Others have defined success as doing something ordinary extraordinarily well.

In order to achieve success, we must meet certain criteria. Could you succeed at failure? Let's analyze an example.

Subject #1	**Subject #2**
High-school dropout	College graduate
Enthusiastic	Careless
Responsible	Irresponsible
Persistent	Unreliable
Aggressive	Insecure
Organized	Disorganized
Disciplined	Undisciplined
Eager to learn new things	Lacks motivation
Honest	Dishonest

There is no question which one is the achiever. Nevertheless, in order to be a failure, you must adopt certain behavior and exercise it as well. If you behaved like Subject #2 and worked at cultivating those characteristics, you would succeed at creating undesirable outcomes in life. You would succeed at failure.

Not even the level of your education decides your success. A college degree is not guarantee for success. There are many individuals with doctoral degrees who struggle to stay employed all their lives, while some who are high-school dropouts may become millionaires and hire others with doctoral degrees to work for them.

In 2010 a Bloomberg study showed that the number one source of CEOs for S&P 500 companies has been college or high school dropouts. In essence many of the people that have had the greatest influence of our times are either high school or college dropouts.

It is also interesting to note that a survey by the National Federation of State High School Associations determined that high grades in high school or college and high ACT scores are not good predictors of later success in life.

A study by the Ewing Marion Kauffman Foundation also showed that high school dropouts had the biggest increase in rate of business creation in 2010 compared to any other group.

There are also elected members of congress without a formal education making decisions about this country. According to the congressional research service published in March 1, 2011, 26 members of the US house and 1 senator do not have an educational degree beyond high school diploma with no mention as to how many of them actually have a high school diploma.

It's almost as if people's achievements were the result of life's recipe and not of formal education. If you wanted to be a successful musician, you could study the biography of a musician you admire and duplicate that pattern. You could practice the same numbers of hours each day, adopt a similar lifestyle, mental attitude, and the same level of confidence. You would undoubtedly become an above-average successful musician.

If you want a successful relationship, read about the requirements for one, create a strategy, and follow the suggestions given by those who already have successful relationships.

That principle is the one used when we go to college to develop a career. If you wish to become an engineer, you're given a recipe to follow. If you do, you'll become and engineer, not a lawyer, because that's a different recipe. Similarly, if you follow the recipe of Subject #1, you'll be an achiever, not a loser. Any recipe you follow, based on someone else's experiences of success or failure, will give you that result.

It's important to put undesirable outcomes in perspective. People who tend to feel like failures are the ones who refuse to learn from their mistakes. They know what makes them feel like a failure, and they know what to do to feel successful, but they don't act. By definition, they become failures.

If you set high standards that you have no intention of pursuing, you're setting yourself up to fail. Although the correlation between success and financial wealth is real, it doesn't mean that someone who doesn't have great wealth is a failure. If you believe that money doesn't define success, you could be the richest man in the world and still feel like a total failure. If you don't have money and decide you're successful just being free of illness, then you'll feel successful. It all depends on how you shape your belief system.

You could be a housewife, plumber, carpenter, or farmer and feel more successful and happier than someone who owns a castle and has millions of dollars in the bank if that person that has a lot of money does not find satisfaction in having a lot of money. There's no relationship between financial success and depression. You can be super rich and feel extremely depressed and suicidal for what you have defined as success or you can be poor and feel successful and not depressed for what you defined as success. Through your belief system only you can decide what success is, and only you can decide how to feel about it.

In short, financial success isn't a tool for overcoming depression. Overcoming depression is the result of a positive state of mind.

Learning to Set Goals

To fulfill life, you must struggle. To struggle is to exist. The homeless struggle in the streets to find food, and they endure many health problems. However, they have goals to find food and get better. The sick ones struggle just to get up and walk. The goal is to get back to normal. The rich struggle to keep their empires intact or to build them bigger.

To struggle is to work toward the achievement of a goal. Goals are the natural objective of life. They're not an option. The mind thrives on goals and achievements. Even a baby's mind, which can't rationalize thought, has a goal. Babies crawl to reach and touch a pleasant-looking object across the room. They cry to get food when they're hungry, and they sit still to rest. They do not rationalize any of the goals, it is human nature. When the mind stops pursuing goals, it can be declared dead.

It's important to learn how to set goals. We mustn't let circumstances set them for us. We should be in charge of choosing them. When we set goals, we can't allow them to become life-or-death obsessions, where we consider suicide if we don't achieve a particular goal. Instead we must use goals to experience a sense of purpose, not to satisfy our selfish desires.

It's also important to learn to appreciate the fact that when we take steps to accomplish a goal, we move ahead. With every step we gain we experience a sense of accomplishment. For that reason, we must be careful not to categorize achievements that come from our decisions, as right or wrong. Right and wrong are the result of thoughts. Making an unfavorable decision isn't wrong. It just means we have something to learn. Favorable decisions mean we have chosen the right path but could later choose a wrong one.

It's important for our belief system to use unfavorable outcomes as a building block for our next attempt and not to feel defeated. Such things shouldn't become roadblocks in our lives. There are no perfect decisions, nor are there perfect outcomes.

If we decide to take on a new job, we begin to realize there are difficulties ahead. We can use those difficulties to develop our experience and gain success, or do nothing and get fired. The same can be said about relationships and careers.

The best part about making decisions is that even if you get fired from a job because of a bad decision, it's not a dead end. If you pursue goals to experience a sense of purpose, not to justify your existence, getting fired can start a new adventure.

If you set yourself the goal of getting a job and succeeding in it, thinking it's the only thing that'll make your life worthwhile, if you're fired, you'll feel sorry for yourself for a long time because that is how your belief system is shaped. You might quit exploring new opportunities or adventures. Worse, if you become obsessed about feeling a sense of defeat for not having achieved the goal that you cherished, you might end up feeling suicidal. If you instead choose to explore new opportunities and adventures with great passion you may end up like many others that have attained a level of success they never dreamed of.

When we pursue goals, every stop is an accomplishment. If we don't achieve our desired result, we haven't failed. In the process, we learned important lessons that give experience for a better attempt next time.

CHAPTER 3

Coping With Depression and Feelings of Suicide

Learning To Work With Our Emotions When Facing Clinical Depression

During symptomatic depression, feelings of grief, guilt, anger, hopelessness, helplessness, and worthlessness can sometimes be so intense they're hard to ignore. It's like having a stalker standing 10 feet away and he is there regardless of where you go. And you know that he is doing this because he wants to make you feel like you do not deserve to live.

Because of your belief system thoughts that you do not deserve to live continue to hound you. As I mentioned earlier, it is not that you hear voices telling you this. If you do hear voices you could be experiencing a different type of mental health challenge and you should probably see a professional. What I mean is that those thoughts of not finding value in life are entrenched in feelings of grief, guilt, anger, hopelessness, helplessness, and worthlessness. You relentlessly experience all these feelings at once and you do not know how to stop them. Nothing motivates you.

That's especially true when you're too attached to an incident that triggers a deep sense of responsibility. In situations like that you might not have the energy to redirect those feelings toward productive thinking. You want to give up.

Under those circumstances, it's important to get in touch with your despair and externalize your feelings as much as possible. The more practical your approach, the more in touch you'll be with your emotions. That may let you gain control over your feelings and maintain a good emotional balance.

One of the most useful approaches to cope with mental depression is to work with your emotions to modify your belief system. It's productive to talk, write, read about, and listen to your feelings. When possible, read over what you've written or tape record yourself and listen to your words.

While in this state, you might have no motivation. You could feel extremely sorry for yourself. However, if you're truly interested in overcoming your depression, you'll take action. You can't let negative emotions run your life. If you do, you become a prisoner of your thoughts.

If your destructive feelings are too overwhelming, and you find yourself crying for no apparent reason, or if you go from happiness to despair, it's important to seek professional help so that you can externalize those feelings.

It's healthy to pay a professional to listen to your situation, especially if you're overwhelmed by feelings of self-destruction and low self-esteem. Find a social worker, psychologist, or psychiatrist who can provide good insight into your feelings. If, after the eighth visit you don't feel you're getting anywhere, find someone else. Specialized degrees don't always mean someone is a good therapist. Social workers were almost always more helpful to me than psychiatrists.

Concentrate on finding a therapist who is very receptive and perceptive to your feelings and needs. If you don't feel you can afford a good professional counselor, and you don't have anyone to talk to, try talking to your pet or into a tape recorder. At least you'll get to listen to yourself and can create a better perspective of your situation. The main objective is to get those feelings out of your system.

You can also externalize your feelings by discussing your problem with friends you trust. Let your friends know you're hurting. That could help you learn more about yourself. They may've noticed a behavioral pattern in you that you don't see, and their input can help you work with your depression or modify your belief system in a more productive way.

If your friends aren't receptive, don't take it badly and assume they don't care. Chances are they don't feel qualified to help you or are going through a rough time, too. However, even if you don't feel they can help, don't stay away from them. Use your friends as a vehicle to take you away from your destructive thoughts. Spend time with them, even if it's a short period of time. Stay as long as your emotional state allows you to enjoy their company without having to talk to them about your issues. That will reduce the amount of time you'll spend entertaining your negative feelings and help you recharge your emotional batteries.

Dealing with the Anger Within

Although you may not realize it, the more prevalent and dominant feeling in a suicidal state is anger. Anger seeks to destroy. On occasions, you may feel the urge to destroy yourself or your surroundings. Simultaneously, you know that none of that will resolve your situation. The more you talk, listen, write, and read over your feelings, the more you'll see how irrational your thinking or belief system is when you're depressed. Your thinking disturbs your emotional balance.

If you decide to describe your feelings, don't consider it a chore. Think of it as a revealing experience. Describe your feelings and see if you're in touch with them. Many times, you'll realize that even when you thought you were clear on something, it'll be difficult to describe in writing or by speaking.

If you write about your feelings you will find out how clear you are about your thoughts. If you cannot describe your thoughts in paper you might not be very clear. Start by writing a letter to yourself. Write about anger and the void in your life. Write about the person who died within you.

If at some point you feel that what you've been describing about your feeling is irrational, do it more accurately. Doing that consistently sometimes brings you to the point where your self-defeating feelings become dull and monotonous. This could be an indication that you are finally succeeding at modifying your belief system.

You might find nothing to write or say when you feel depressed. That's the time when you can start working in a more productive, efficient manner. Start talking, listening, writing, and reading about how you want things to be. Work on the benefits of confronting the situation in a more constructive manner. It's imperative that you start asking yourself what you expect to accomplish by dwelling in something over which you may not have control.

In addition to the way you feel during depression, there are factors in your surroundings that can intensify your emotions or bring on worse depression. If you monitor your feelings carefully, you may begin to realize that certain surroundings make you depressed.

You might find you get depressed if you're in a room with dull walls, no decorations, and poor lighting. There's nothing to focus on but your emotional issues.

Conversely, it might be difficult to feel depressed when you walk through a park filled with gardens on a cool sunny day. Everywhere you look, the beauty of nature captures your emotions. The scenery is so expressive that it's hard to concentrate on anything else.

Our senses are the key to determining how depressed we feel. Whatever is pleasant to your eyes, ears, nose, and skin can be pleasant to your mind, no matter how much guilt or grief you've been feeling. Taking a warm shower after crying for hours may bring relief because through your skin your mind associate warm water with a pleasant and relaxing feeling. Looking at pictures that remind you of good times can reinforce the idea that you weren't always unhappy. Through your eyes, your mind awakens feelings that you thought were dead. Walking through places where people gather to have fun helps divert your attention from yourself also.

If you feel grief over the death of a loved one, you might be able to comfort yourself by looking at that person's picture and writing a letter, stating all the things you never had a chance to say. Continue until you've described all your feelings.

It's important to learn to identify every element that provides a positive stimulus to your mind and use them. Create a list of things that give you pleasure and try to keep them accessible for the times when you need them. Consider your visual, auditory, physical, and olfactory senses when you make your list.

Keep in mind that you control your environment most of the time. You can change it if you choose, or you can stay away from it if you can't change it. You can make your home or room provide a pleasant environment by decorating and lighting it to your satisfaction.

Close your eyes and concentrate on the things that could make your home or room more positive. List those things and work toward making them real.

You must also note the elements in your surroundings that provide negative feelings, precipitating sadness, guilt, or anger and work to eliminate them. If you work at a job where your superiors don't show any appreciation for your accomplishments can make you angry and lower your self-esteem. Similarly, a visit to your family might bring out negative emotions.

By becoming aware of those things, you learn to prepare yourself to reach for the positive things whenever your mood starts deteriorating. Determine how to minimize the negative experiences. Limit your exposure to events that make you uncomfortable and prepare a support environment or group for afterwards, or be more assertive.

If you are at home and have a bad interaction with your family, it might be the wrong idea to go to your apartment and sit there alone. It would be more productive to go to a park and sit in a bench while you process your feelings. You can also visit a good friend or treat yourself to a nice meal.

By becoming acquainted with how your emotions

work, you can take control of them. That's a key factor for overcoming depression. The more you learn about your feelings, the less likely it'll be that you lose control over your life.

Let me give you an example. If you're getting ready to watch a movie you've been waiting anxiously for, you might get angry or anxious if the TV set breaks down right at the start of the movie. If you knew how to repair it, you could fix the problem and continue. That would give you control of the situation. In that case the incident with the TV set won't affect your emotions.

We need to work with feelings in a similar manner. When you start feeling depressed, look at what's causing it and work to counter those emotions with positive ones. Learn to repair your emotions as you would a TV. You can do this if you get to know yourself well.

There are many ways of controlling your feelings. It's unfortunate that the happy scenes in alcohol commercials lead people to believe that alcohol will help us with sadness or depression. Alcohol is the most common resource to which people turn. However it is also the reason I attempted suicide. I had a few drinks at a bar and in an instant suicide looked like a very realistic solution to my depression. When I was sober, I was always reluctant about committing suicide because the effect it would have on my loved ones.

Unfortunately, the commercials never show how drinking can motivate you to commit suicide or tear your family apart and destroy your future. They never show how alcohol deteriorates the body and makes many people adopt disgusting behaviors. It's unfortunate that jogging, writing, or other activities aren't considered profitable enough to promote them as a resource for a happy life.

The number of activities you can perform to enrich your lack of motivation depends on your interests and creativity. You can walk, run, or exercise to express anger and frustration. You can play a musical instrument to express guilt. Those and others you come up with can help externalize your feelings.

Every time you're successful at externalizing your feelings, you'll experience a sense of relief from your emotional pressure. It's important that your list of activities be as extensive as possible, because, when you feel depressed, it's easy to get bored. If you have few interests, don't try them all at the same time and place every day. Be creative and use variety.

If you like to write, use different colored pens and choose a color that suits your mood for the day. If you swim, try a different stroke from the one you used last time. If you walk or run, choose a different route every day. Eliminate anything that feels like routine.

Always be creative in your activities, and try at least one activity every day. Force yourself even if you're not in the mood. If you have twenty hours to think about your emotional issues, you'll spend twenty hours on them, but that doesn't mean you'll resolve anything. Resolution might be more difficult, because you're too emotionally drained to come up with fresh ideas on how to overcome your situation. If you redirect your attention to other activities, you'll bring in a new perspective later.

If you know the elements that affect your emotions, you can learn to gain control over them. If you do, you'll eventually eliminate unhealthy feelings from your life and create a stronger belief system.

When you first reveal a personal tragedy to someone, it might be difficult to contain your emotions, and you might burst into tears. The more you exercise your emotions by talking and writing about them, the easier it is to discuss them. Eventually, you might find yourself telling the same story to a crowd, who watch you with admiration for sharing it with such strength. If you find yourself in that situation, you either have conquered your feelings of depression or you are close to doing it.

Let's Talk Suicide

Once you've found yourself in a state of deep depression for a while, you might give up hope of experiencing anything better. You lose your faith for anything that might help. You feel tired of the challenges in life, and there seems to be no reason to continue your existence.

At that point, suicide might seem like the only way out. That's a signal that you must work to modify your belief system and do whatever it takes to change your patterns and thoughts. You can do that by carefully filtering or analyzing your feelings about suicide. Start by reflecting about the fact that the Earth is several billion years old, and you've only glimpsed a tiny portion of it.

If you're lucky, you will have one hundred years to live. Your life is like a grain of sand. Out of all possible grains that could glimpse the world, you're one of them. Your only duty is to contribute to it with your joys, pains, intellect, and suffering.

It's also your duty to witness the universe and understand that you're the one person who can contribute to its mystery by challenging the odds everyone faces against living their lives fully. The moment we're born, we begin dying. The odds of dying are high. Everything we do in our lives must be done to help us continue living.

Keep in mind that the world's story is complex and fascinating. It's complex, because it's based on what people and nature did to get us where we are today. It's fascinating, because before we got there, a cycle of destruction and reconstruction occurred. Without them we wouldn't have learned what was necessary in order to be where we are and move on.

Take for example those who died as the result of famine. They did as much for humanity as any other major breakthrough that took place in history. When it first occurred, famine gave a different dimension to our existence. Those who died taught everyone an invaluable lesson about what happens when society doesn't become self sufficient. No one would've taken any steps if someone had told them to. People had to witness it. Many nations now know what must be done to prevent famine.

In the minds of famine victims, it's possible that they didn't feel live was worth living when they died. However, they are remembered collectively as part of world's history. Through them the world learned about the importance of preventing famine. They did not die in vain.

Everyone plays a significant role in the world whether he suffers or succeeds. It's only a matter of being able to accept your role in life and play it to your best and fight to change what you don't like and celebrate the things you do. If you want to change the only thing limiting you is your mind.

After thinking about all that, answer or, if possible, write an essay on the following questions:

Would happiness mean anything if sadness didn't exist? Define happiness without alluding to sadness.

How would you appreciate success if you never experience failure? Define success without alluding to failure.

Would there be any reason to have a job or to study if there were no human needs? If we didn't have needs, how could we develop our intellect?

How would you define love if hate were unknown? Define love without alluding to hate.

Is there any reason for faith if despair didn't exist?

If you believe in God, what's the purpose of God if evil doesn't exist?

Would it be possible for heroes or governments to exist if malicious intent and tragic events didn't exist?

Could there be any need for fun if we didn't

experience sadness?

What is humanity's purpose if pain, needs, and malicious intent didn't exist, diseases couldn't develop, failure was impossible, and sadness and crime didn't exist? If none of those existed, would humanity's purpose be greater than that of other mammalian species?

Without our ability to experience those things, we would be on the planet roaming the world with no purpose. Is humanity's purpose found within imperfection?

After you answer or write assays about all those questions, ask yourself if your present situation fulfills the purpose of life. If you ended your life, would you be destroying its purpose?

We should also evaluate life's fairness. If the life of a humble person ends violently, we call it tragic and unfair. If a hard core criminal dies that way, we call it a punishment well deserved and justified. Is death that doesn't come about suicide a punishment or the fulfillment of life's purpose?

Read through those questions and then explain what you expect to accomplish through suicide. Perhaps you expect to end your pain. Remember that pain is the source of change in our lives. Pain brought technology and science to their current levels and will contribute to their breakthroughs for as long as pain exists.

Every emotional or physical pain provides us with the objective of our existence. Every person who experienced pain and suffering in the past contributed to making our lives less painful, which, in turn, contributes to a more sophisticated society.

For every scientific breakthrough, there was a need or pain to be lived. Otherwise, they wouldn't be called breakthroughs. Depending on how painful certain emotional issues are in society it will decide how our lifestyles will change.

It's important to remember that if people committed suicide every time they felt physical or emotional pain, our race would be extinct.

Taking action to avoid pain is part of our nature. If you took a shower, and boiling water came from the showerhead, you would jump out to avoid getting burned. When you're hungry, you take action to relieve your hunger.

If someone goes around a community causing pain to others, society bands together to make sure that person is caught and punished. Pain has been the architect of all the laws in every society in the world. They were created to minimize pain.

Unfortunately, we, as individuals, take pain for granted and ignore the fact that it has made our existence more enjoyable. We don't want to pay the price of the changing process. We prefer others pay, and we spend our lives avoiding the painful process of change.

Even though you might feel that by committing suicide you could end your pain, the truth is that committing suicide just to end pain is hard to justify because it is necessary for self-worth. You wouldn't have a sense of purpose unless you had to relieve pain in your life.

In addition, tiredness from enduring pain is another reason people consider suicide. I disagree with that. If someone were terminally ill, it would be reasonable to think he was tired of fighting his destiny. However, even that does not justify suicide. The fulfillment of life is only found in death that is not self-inflicted.

However, if someone feels lonely, because he lacks social skills, someone else is fired from a job, or someone ends a relationship, would it be fatigue from enduring pain that urges them to commit suicide? You might be tired simply from having depression, which drains one's energy. Subconsciously, you probably feel anger against yourself. It is important to become aware at that point that your belief system is directing that anger.

If you dig into your own thoughts, you might also realize something more serious than tiredness is occurring. It's possible that you feel you failed to overcome the situation or failed to learn the lesson you've been trying to teach yourself. That could bring the urge for self-punishment.

Because of your belief system, you might feel you deserve to die for not being capable of getting what you want out of life. You might feel like a child who can't understand what someone is teaching him. If your peers lost patience with you when you didn't understand something, you might lose patience with yourself when you feel you failed to improve on something that seems simple. By modifying your belief system you might avoid dealing with such thoughts.

Learning to Remain Productive When Experiencing Feelings of Suicide

It is important to feel you can remain productive when you're depressed. Set a small daily goal which you can accomplish even if you're crying. That might include cleaning your apartment, washing the car, writing letters, cooking three meals a day, doing laundry, walking a few miles, watching an inspirational movie, or reading a fun book. Don't let self-defeating feelings stalk you and dictate your productivity or your accomplishments in life. Prove to yourself you, not circumstance, are in charge of your feelings no matter how much pain you have. Make an effort to feel needed and appreciated by others.

You can accomplish that by volunteering for a cause to which you believe. If you enjoy the company of adults, volunteer to help the elderly. If you like kids, work with them. If you're not comfortable around people work with pets. Those activities let you look at problems from a different perspective. You will also limit the amount of time you spend worrying about your issues.

There's nothing productive about worrying for hours every day over something you didn't achieve. Worrying about a way to relieve your emotional pain accomplishes nothing.

Only people who take action accomplish something. You can't change your emotional state by worrying; you change it by taking action. When you feel you've reached bottom, every step you take has to go up. That's the key to success. To have success, it is best to fail in many ways first. Once you've experienced many failures, success may be the only alternative.

If you feel strongly about committing suicide, think about the people you care about. Even if you feel that your family truly does not care about you there are others that do but you may not even know it because you are too conflicted to believe it. I'm sure you don't want to put them through what you're experiencing. If you take your own life, others will endure feelings of guilt, helplessness, hopelessness, and despair at a much higher level than you ever experienced it.

You should feel proud about the fact that you're having difficulties, because you've got the experience and stamina to deal with them.

You can always use suicidal feelings to your advantage. If there's nothing to live for, there are many things to die for. Mahatma Gandhi and Martin Luther King Jr., are examples of people who were willing to die for their beliefs. There are thousands of organizations that could use someone willing to die for a good cause.

Become useful to the people who need your talent, intellect, experience, or existence. If you don't fear death, you can turn that into your biggest asset and make significant contributions to society. Don't deprive others of the value of your life.

You can also take advantage of your feelings and try to achieve the good things in life you never attempted, because you thought they'd keep you from enjoying other things, or you feared failure. When nothing matters, rejection becomes meaningless and failure doesn't count.

If you feel hurt along the way, be glad. That means

you still care about yourself---something you assumed wasn't important. Challenge yourself to keep moving and find out how much more you might care about yourself. If you fail or get rejected and don't feel anything be glad. That means you can move on and keep trying the good things in life you never tried before.

At the end of your journey, if you haven't enjoyed any of it, your experience will become the foundation of your strength for future challenges.

It's possible you're considering suicide as a way of punishing the person who caused you pain. If that's true, ask yourself if the person will ever have a fair chance to correct his mistake once you're dead. You might cause more pain to that person than what you felt. Relationships, jobs, anger, and mistakes are transient things. They can be replaced or corrected --- your life can't.

When considering suicide, be aware of the fact that suicidal feelings are ambivalent. Part of you wants to live, another part wants to die. You've let the part that wants to die dominate the other part.

If your feelings about committing suicide are too strong, give yourself an extra day to think things over before attempting it. In the meantime, sort out your feelings and describe their objective. There's nothing more valuable than filtering or reasoning through feelings that might otherwise sap your energy and weaken your will to live.

Only when you succeed at that will you be able to work towards making the part of you that wants to live bigger than the part that wants to die. As I said, do it by restructuring your feelings or your belief system.

Helping Someone who's Suicidal

Always be perceptive with the people with whom you interact. Your acquaintances, friends, or relatives will seldom admit they're feeling suicidal. The same applies to crisis agencies, where the clients don't express their feelings, either.

People who are considering suicide will give you subtle messages to let you know it's on their mind. There are behavioral and verbal clues through which a person lets you know he's feeling suicidal.

Verbal Clues

I'm tired of my life.
I don't care about anything anymore.
Nothing matters anymore
I won't be around much longer.
I have nothing to live for.
I'm happy now!
My problems will be over soon.

Behavioral Clues

Giving away valued possessions
Buying a weapon while depressed
Making out a will
A sudden and unexplained recovery from depression
Changes in behavioral patterns – sex, sleep, work, study, or alcohol use.
Frequent and sudden crying
Quitting a job that he or she used to love
In a subtle way he or she appears to be saying goodbye

Through those clues, a person is making assertions that reflect feelings of anger, worthlessness, and frustration. The only way you can tell if someone feels suicidal is by asking them bluntly. Never be afraid to ask that of anyone. You won't give them the idea. The concept of suicide has been around for centuries, and you aren't providing a new alternative to someone—they already know about it.

The main reason people feel reluctant to discuss and admit suicidal thoughts is because society overall doesn't appreciate such people. Those who commit suicide are considered cowards or cheats by some.

When someone admits to feeling suicidal, he may be more exposed to rejection, negative remarks, and ridicule. Never make such people feel stupid, act as if suicide was a horrible thing to do, become shocked, tell him he can't, question his state of mind, or argue about the moral aspects of suicide. More importantly do not treat them as if they were manipulating you because they want attention. The truth of the matter is that at this very moment they need attention.

As such, thank the person for trusting you enough to discuss it. Be open and supportive of the person's feelings regardless of how insignificant the problem seems. Never encourage someone to commit suicide even if you feel they have good reason. Establish the lethality of the situation. If the person has no idea how he might go about committing suicide, the lethality is low. If he's got a careful plan or is in the midst of trying it---if he already took the pills or is holding a gun---- the lethality is high. Take the situation seriously and make sure proper steps are taking to save his life.

Once you're certain the person is safe, talk openly to him about his feelings of suicide. Listen, empathize, be supportive, and be understanding. Stay for as long as that person needs you.

When you start a conversation with someone who's considering suicide, it increases in intensity and then decreases. The person becomes more relaxed, which indicates he's accepting his situation more easily. To make sure that's true, check back with the person. Ask how he's feeling and if he's still suicidal. If he says he's feeling better, don't leave. Instead, discuss things that made him feel happy in the past, things that he enjoys talking about, his dreams and goals. If he has dreams and goals that's a good sign. He may have something to live for. If he doesn't have any dreams or goals talk about the things he would like to do in the short and long term. Be supportive of his ideas and suggest ways to make them real.

Since people who feel suicidal are ambivalent about

life, while part of them still wants to live, work to make that part stronger. Use positive thoughts and supportiveness in your conversation. If the person starts talking with enthusiasm, point it out and make him realize he can feel enthusiastic any time he wants by entertaining positive thoughts.

Tell him to restructure his thinking toward more positive thoughts and reinforce your words by giving value to the positive aspects of his life. As long as he lives, there's a chance he'll have better times again. If he commits suicide, that'll never happen.

Before you leave, make sure you check what kind of emotional support he's got. If possible, offer ideas on how to seek additional support. At the end of the conversation, make a contract in which the person agrees to contact you before attempting suicide. Encourage the person to seek professional help.

Always remember the act of suicide is a personal choice. I attempted suicide not because I felt my family did not love me or because no one wanted to help me, nor because I felt hated by others. I attempted suicide because I wanted to be at peace. I wanted my mind to stop having relentless thoughts and feelings of despair, hopelessness, helplessness, and worthlessness.

Thus, never blame yourself for someone's suicide. If the person thought you had the solution, he would've let you know. When someone is convinced no one can help, it wouldn't matter what you did. You'd never be able to help.

The only way such people can be helped is if they believe they can be helped. If they're not willing to listen to you or accept your help, they'll commit suicide if they wish. No one else is responsible for their lives. No one should make you feel guilty about their deaths, even if they gave you a chance to help.

You're a human being with your own problems and limitations not God. If you couldn't help, there were other sources they could've considered before committing such an act. Never carry such guilt. It would not be fair.

As I mentioned earlier a person that commits suicide is only trying to achieve a sense of peace that he thinks he can no longer achieve because he is too tired to keep trying. Generally, people that attempt or commit suicide know that any improvement in their mood through interaction with their family or friends will be short lived and that they'll be back feeling desponded again sooner than later. This is the sense of peace that I wanted to achieve when I attempted suicide. I had convinced myself that any improvement in my mood was not going to be worth it because I was going to be back in a rot again in no time.

However, after surviving my suicide attempt I decided not to dump my emotional pain onto the shoulders of my loved ones by killing myself. That would not have been fair. As such, I am alive today because I decided to assume responsibility for my pain and found a way to work with it. If I had not done that I would have died by my own hands regardless of what anyone did to help me appreciate life.

CHAPTER 4

A word about Families, Their Influence on Our Emotional Strength, and Our Ability to Change

Who's Responsible for Our Ability to Change?

Depression can be considered a symptom of poor emotional development. The way we're raised by parents and family is a key to how successful we'll be when we confront challenges. Some parents prefer reverse psychology to motivate their children. It's all too familiar when a child brings home bad grades for some parents and peers to call him stupid, inept, or a moron, hoping the child will accept the challenge of proving them wrong.

Another typical situation is where the parents don't give more respect to the child than to a pet. Some parents assume the kid's too young and don't know much yet, so they can't be reasoned with. They feel their only alternative is to spank them when they misbehave as if dealing with a pet or even less than a pet. After all we all know that some pets can be taught to behave better without having to resort to physical punishment. Anyone who believes that children are smarter than pets should be able to understand that children can be taught to behave better without having to resort to physical punishment.

Another scenario is where parents sexually abuse their children, believing they aren't old enough to get hurt by such despicable behavior.

Some parents may also look back on their own history of failure and assume their children are destined to the same fate. Thus, they don't put any faith in them or provide the proper support for them to take on successful challenges.

Other parents believe they should distant from their children and never reveal their emotions so that they can get their children's respect. They don't want to appear weak and try to portray a strong personality in front of the children.

Those parenting approaches may create children with a belief system that is drenched in low self-esteem and self-destructive behavior. Most times the end result is that the children may rebel against their parents. When those scenarios are filled with extreme situations of neglect, violence, alcoholism, and emotional, physical, and sexual abuse, they create emotionally unstable individuals.

Occasionally, a member of the family or the community has a positive influence on the child and counteracts the effects of his environment. If the child never meets anyone who can help, he may never learn to appreciate or respect his life or the lives of others.

As such, your past can significantly influence your emotional state as an adult. However, if you insist on holding onto your memories, you accomplish only one thing---you refuse to accept the fact that you're responsible for your present situation. When you were growing up, your peers influenced your personality and belief system, but, once you were capable of making changes in your belief system, then it's your responsibility. It's never too late to learn new skills. The resources are waiting for you to make up your mind to use them. The limitations you face are the result of your thoughts.

You might think your past experiences with your family are responsible for your high or low self-esteem. Most people believe that you can only have positive self-esteem if you had positive experiences as a child. However, if you study the lives of people who have achieved remarkable things, you'll find many had very negative lives growing up. High self-esteem isn't dependent on positive or negative experiences only. It is dependent on the meaning you give to them. It is dependent on how you shape up your belief system.

If you view your negative experiences as things to keep in mind to influence your decisions in becoming a better person, you have high self-esteem. If you view them as a reflection of who you are, you'll probably have low self-esteem. Whether you view those experiences as lessons or a reflection of yourself depends on the type of thoughts you entertain.

In order to change the idea that the past controls your life, you must accept the fact that your thoughts may try to avoid taking responsibility for your present situation. You must modify your belief system and restructure your thinking by challenging those thoughts. Reject your negative self-image and promote positive thoughts.

CHAPTER 5

Medication, Food, and You

The Partial Answer to Some of Your Mood Changes

Monitoring the way you feel after taking certain medications and foods is the best way to avoid any biochemical imbalance that could make you depressed. When I monitor my mood in response to activities, food, and medication, I feel the effect those things have on my emotional health.

When I look back to my childhood, I can identify which things contributed to my withdrawn attitude. One factor concerned medication I took for my allergies and asthma-like condition. I was always in poor health as a kid, with chronic respiratory conditions, and the physician suggested I take antihistamines and decongestants daily. That continued until I went to college.

What I didn't realize then was the drowsiness effects of the antihistamines and the mood swings that decongestants caused when taken with antihistamines. Although it's believed that the body is able to eventually tolerate that, it's not always true. It depends on individual physiology.

In my case, the side effects were constant. Antihistamines didn't just make me sleepy, they made me act withdrawn because I felt exhausted and sleepy and because I was also taking decongestants, my vulnerable mood swings were frequent. That opened the door for bullies to target me.

If, as many experts believe, depression comes from a biochemical imbalance, it could've been induced in me by the constant presence of such drugs in my brain. It's easy for me to understand it now, but, back then, I was confused. I'd been in psychotherapy since early age, but never heard the term clinical depression. Thus, I didn't know I was experiencing symptoms associated with that disease until I was diagnosed with it later in life.

Until then, I thought I was being treated for shyness and other behavioral problems. Thus, I kept taking the medications until I realized how much they contributed to my negative feelings.

When I began graduate school, and my depression became even worse, I visited a social worker who told me what the symptoms of clinical depression were. That was when I began to understand what was wrong with me. From that point on I began my journey out of the labyrinth.

Soon after that, I studied and monitored the effect medications had on my mood. I asked my physician to prescribe antihistamines that wouldn't make me feel drowsy, withdrawn, or even depressed. After I did that I began to function better, but I'd been taking the mood altering drugs for a long time and, thus, getting to understand my emotions was a struggle.

Another factor that may have contributed to my clinical depression as a child was my diet. I didn't like the food in middle school and skipped lunch every day. I remember those days vividly. I was underweight and felt weak, irritable, anxious, and exhausted. I couldn't enjoy school activities. This also opened the door for bullies to target me. When I began monitoring how diet affected my depression, I realized my own ignorance contributed to my problem.

Today, I carefully monitor how my mood changes with diet. Although hundreds of books have been written about that, there are several things on which all experts agree.

Don't skip a meal.
Eat a well-balanced diet.
Avoid eating snacks containing refined sugar if you have an empty stomach.
Eat meals rich in protein and polyunsaturated fats.
Take your daily requirement of vitamins and minerals if you

are a picky eater.

To avoid becoming overweight the calories you eat on a day are more important than the type of diet you choose to follow.

Your diet should be designed so that it won't alter your insulin level too much. Glucose is the main source of energy for the brain. When your diet is rich in refined sugars that triggers an increase in blood insulin levels that may remain high even when the blood sugar goes back down to normal. As a result, the glucose levels in your blood continue to drop, inducing a temporary hypoglycemic state that leaves your brain without much energy. As such, you may experience drastic mood changes.

That's why dietitians recommend you eat a diet rich in protein and complex carbohydrates, because those foods won't induce drastic increases in blood levels of insulin, and provide the brain with the appropriate amount of sugar.

It's important to design a diet that caters positively to your mood. It's a bad idea to blindly accept some expert's suggestion without seeing if it would be beneficial for you.

Although some experts suggest it's better to eat several small meals throughout the day instead of three large ones, I found that my stomach feels unsettled throughout the day when I do that and so does my mood.

Similarly some experts suggest you eat lunches that are rich in tyrosine but have no carbohydrates. Carbohydrates are a good source of tryptophan, the source of the neurotransmitter serotonin, which relaxes, slows you down, and helps you sleep. Tyrosine increases the levels of dopamine and norepinephrine, which are chemical messengers that help you, stay alert.

However, when I eat a diet rich in protein or tyrosine I feel somewhat edgy. When I eat a diet rich in protein and then eat a small dessert rich in refine sugar I feel very relaxed and satisfied.

As such, when dealing with depression, it's important to monitor your mood and identify the positive and negative effects of the drugs and foods you eat. Even if your medication and diet aren't responsible for the imbalance of neurotransmitters that make you depressed, you don't want to make your condition worse by having a diet or medication that might contribute to the problem.

CHAPTER 6

Keeping Your Thoughts in Perspective

Activities That Can Help You Keep Your Thoughts in Perspective

If you ever feel imprisoned by feelings of depression, the first thing to keep in mind is that the power of the disease lies in the way it controls your thoughts, which are produced by your belief system. As you seek a solution to clinical depression by seeking professional treatment, you must learn to keep thoughts of hopelessness, worthlessness, and helplessness from stalking you. If you don't do that, you'll have trouble getting the full benefit of your treatment. Psychotherapy sessions usually don't last more than half an hour and are rarely done more than twice a week.

If you don't learn to keep your destructive thoughts away, you'll have endless hours in which to entertain self-defeating, destructive thoughts. The benefits of psychotherapy sessions won't last long if you keep thinking in old patterns.

One of the best ways to prevent depression from controlling your thoughts is to try to modify your belief system and become engaged in activities that influence your mind positively. Every day, for the next thirty days, choose one activity from the following list and pursue it. Choose a new one every day until you complete thirty.

After doing thirty exercises, determine how many you did successfully. Repeat the exercise until your thoughts no longer stalk you

1. Live today as if it were the last day of your life. Take a risk.
2. If you think about a new idea today, think, I'll pursue it, and nothing will stop me from achieving it. Do that every time the idea comes to mind. Take one more

step to achieve it.

3. Do more than you planned to do today.

4. Prioritize what you need to get done today. At the end of the day, make sure you've completed your top priority and enjoy the moment.

5. Write a one page essay about your most desired goals and a recipe on how to achieve them.

6. Commit yourself today to discuss your most desired goals with at least one person who would have some idea of how to achieve them.

7. Create a motto for yourself that reinforces the fact that you appreciate who you are.

8. Look in the mirror and repeat, with great conviction, "I believe in myself," at least until you begin to truly believe what you are saying.

9. Make a list of the way in which you'll compensate yourself for every unacceptable outcome you might achieve today.

10. Make a list of every unacceptable outcome you achieved yesterday, and then create a plan to use those things as stepping stones to achieve positive results today.

11. Close your eyes and visualize the achievement of your most-desired goal. Experience how you'll feel when you achieve it. Feel your heart rate, breathing rate, and state of mind.

12. Learn a relaxation technique that works for you and use it every day.

13. Choose your favorite place to relax and reflect on the good times in your life.

14. On your way home from work or school, visit a park or lake, relax, and watch people go about their lives.

15. Write a one page essay about what you stand for and how you'd like to be remembered. Make it a point to read the essay every morning before going to school or work. Modify and improve your essay as you see fit.

16. Make a point of pleasing no one but you for the next thirty days. Read the biography of Thomas Edison and learn the benefits of living to make yourself happy. When you're happy, everyone around you feels good about you.

17. For the next thirty days, spend a few minutes in the morning and evening reviewing, and, if possible, memorizing every statement of a book that inspires you to transform your thoughts.

18. Look at your world with an open mind. Filter your thoughts and identify forces that negatively influence your emotions. Listen to inspiring audio tapes and read the biographies of inspiring people.

19. Break out of your routines. If you usually drive to work, take the bus. If you eat lunch or dinner at the same restaurant every day, eat at different restaurants for the next seven days. If you eat at home, treat yourself for a different dessert every day for seven days. If you listen to the same radio station every day, try a different one every day for thirty days.

20. Find out about organizations that could use you as a volunteer.

21. Tell one of your friends how much you appreciate the friendship.

22. Don't be critical of yourself or anyone for seven days.

23. Do an inventory of your habits and commit yourself to get rid of unhealthy ones.

24. It's been said that success isn't a destination but a journey. Figure out what part of the journey you're pursuing, which are the most difficult ones, and what you need to do to make them easier.

25. Dress well and look alert to show you feel good about yourself.

26. Show your appreciation when others compliment you by responding with a simple, "Thank you."

27. Make the point of making eye contact when talking to someone, especially if you're expressing your opinion on something.

28. Work to become a positive role model for the people who don't believe in your potential.

29. Don't seek to be emotionally rewarded by anyone else but yourself for what you achieve today.

30. Set aside thirty minutes of your day to relax and reflect on what you need to do to respond more effectively to your challenges.

31. List five unpleasant but necessary tasks you must complete and haven't. Set a deadline and do them.

Once completed, feel good about it and reward yourself by treating yourself to a tasty meal or going for a walk at a park or lake.

32. Make a list of the things you plan to achieve today. At the end of the day, classify the outcome of your pursuits as desirable or undesirable. After that, make a list of the things you learned from each type.

33. Make the point of not dwelling on a mistake if you make one today. Someone that hasn't made many errors is not an experienced person.

34. Make a donation to an organization or a person for which you won't be rewarded. Dwell on the satisfaction of doing it.

35. As you walk or drive around today, make it a point to enjoy every living thing you see.

36. Pick one day of the weekend to do something you've never done before. Repeat this exercise once a month.

37. Take the time to prepare a delicious, nutritious breakfast at least once a week. Eat it while listening to inspiring music.

38. Make it a point to praise someone today. Tell him how good you feel about what he does and who he is.

39. As you confront a problem today, rejoice and feel good about the fact that you'll again have the opportunity to deal with a challenge that will improve your existence. The only way we gain experience in our life is by solving problems.

40. Make it a point to talk to someone who's intellectually stimulating and to challenge his thoughts. By doing that, he'll challenge your thoughts as well.

41. Write down at least five negative emotions you're currently experiencing and describe how they prevent you from achieving a sense of personal satisfaction. Be honest with yourself when you do this. Describe why you want to continue entertaining those emotions. If you have no valid reason, make a commitment to release them.

42. Identify any beliefs that continue to prevent you from achieving your desired goals and describe why you continue to entertain them. If there's no valid reason, make a commitment to transform those beliefs by

entertaining a new set that will enable you to achieve your goals. Write them down on a piece of paper and review them every time you catch yourself thinking about your negative beliefs.

43. Write down two situations in which you felt rejected and two where you felt incompetent. Write about the benefits gained from each one.

If you carry out these exercises with enthusiasm and curiosity, by the time you complete the list, you'll probably have made significant progress in modifying your belief system and have learned more about yourself than most people do in a lifetime.

CHAPTER 7

Final Thoughts

I want to remind you that thoughts are the power of our lives and thoughts are driven by our belief system. Who you are and who you become depend on your belief system and the kind of thoughts you entertain. Unfortunately, no one can make that decision but you, because you're the only person who has total control over your thoughts. Whether you allow your belief system to become the stalker within that will destroy your world or the power within that will transform negative outcomes into success depends on you.

The fact that I managed to transform my belief system and consequently my thoughts doesn't mean my life has been without problems. I still have them, but, by achieving my current level of understanding about my thoughts, I have experienced a sense of growing sanity and an understanding of a basic pleasure. There isn't much room in my mind for the belief system that once stalked it. There's only room for life.

I assure you that to let self-defeating destructive thoughts stalk your mind is to die. Even if those thoughts grow and gain control of your life, they can be destroyed. They will only prevail for as long as you let them. Your only limitation, which is also your strength, is that you have absolute control over your decision.